A Witch's Grimoire

⇌ Create Your Own Book of Shadows ⇌

Judy Ann Nock

Adams Media
Avon, Massachusetts

Dedication

Dedicated to the memory of those who have passed on, the love of those who are, and the promise of those yet to be.

Copyright © 2005, F+W Publications, Inc.
All rights reserved. This book, or parts thereof, may not be reproduced in any form without permission from the publisher; exceptions are made for brief excerpts used in published reviews.

Provenance Press® is a registered trademark of F+W Publications, Inc.
Provenance Press®, an imprint of Adams Media.
57 Littlefield Street
Avon, MA 02322
www.adamsmedia.com

ISBN 10: 1-59337-407-0
ISBN 13: 978-1-59337-407-5

Printed in Canada
J I H G F E D C B

Library of Congress Cataloging-in-Publication Data
Nock, Judy Ann.
A witch's grimoire / Judy Ann Olsen.
p. cm.
Includes bibliographical references.
ISBN 1-59337-407-0
1. Witchcraft--Handbooks, manuals, etc. 2. Magic--Handbooks, manuals, etc. I. Title.

BF1566.O48 2005
133.4'3--dc22

2005011020

This publication is designed to provide accurate and authoritative information with regard to the subject matter covered. It is sold with the understanding that the publisher is not engaged in rendering legal, accounting, or other professional advice. If legal advice or other expert assistance is required, the services of a competent professional person should be sought.

—From a *Declaration of Principles* jointly adopted by a Committee of the American Bar Association and a Committee of Publishers and Associations

Many of the designations used by manufacturers and sellers to distinguish their products are claimed as trademarks. Where those designations appear in this book and Adams Media was aware of a trademark claim, the designations have been printed with initial capital letters.

Contents

Acknowledgments   vii

Introduction   ix

Chapter One: Book of Memory   1
From Days of Old: What Is a Grimoire?   1
The Journey Begins: Why Should You Write a Grimoire?   4
Carved in Stone: Where Does the Grimoire Come From?   5
Begin at the Beginning: Choose Your Book   9
Craft Your Own: Make the Grimoire from Scratch   10
Consecrate Your Grimoire: As It Is Written, Let It Be Done   18

Chapter Two: Book of Foundation   25
Steps on the Wiccan Path   26
Create Sacred Space   29
Cast the Circle Thrice About   32
Craft Your Invocations   35
Awakening the Elemental Powers   39
Open the Circle   47

Chapter Three: Book of Changes   55
Magic: Theory and Practice   56
The Magical Tools   58
Consecrate Your Working Tools   64
Put Theory into Practice   66
Craft Your Own Spells   73

Chapter Four: Book of Visions 79
- Creative Visualization 80
- The Chakras 88
- Meditation 96
- Touch Sound 98

Chapter Five: Book of Days 103
- Sunday 104
- Monday 104
- Tuesday 105
- Wednesday 106
- Thursday 107
- Friday 107
- Saturday 108
- Morning Rites 109
- Evening Rites 111
- Dreamwork 113
- Record Your Dreams 115
- The Temple Sleep 116
- Dream Interpretations 122

Chapter Six: Book of Lore 135
- The Wiccan Rede 135
- The Charge of the Goddess 137
- The Song of Amergin 139
- The Great Wheel 141
- The Sabbats 142
- Cross-Quarter Days 146
- Esbats 148

Chapter Seven: Book of Transformation 167
Trance: Traveling the Divine Matrix 168
Scrying: Things That Are, That Were, That Shall Be 173
Aspecting: The Goddess Reveals Her Many Faces 180
Channeling: The Goddess Speaks Through You 187

Chapter Eight: Book of Lights and Shadows 191
Candle Magic 192
The Ritual Use of Herbs 197
Sympathetic Magic and the Use of Gems 217
Gemstone Correspondences 219

Chapter Nine: Practical Applications
Walk the Path and Live a Spiritual Life 229
Final Notes 233

Appendix 235
Sources for Obtaining Magical Ingredients 235
Suggested Reading 237
Selected Bibliography 239

Index 244

Acknowledgments

This book was written between August 1 and October 31, 2004, during the second trimester of my first successful pregnancy. It is an amazing experience to have had two lifelong dreams simultaneously come true, and I would like to acknowledge all of the dream builders I have met along the way.

To my family, without whose love and support this undertaking would have seemed impossible, your graciousness, understanding, and acceptance made me believe in myself.

To Gabrielle Lichterman, without whose friendship and support this book quite literally may not have happened. To June Clark, Danielle Chiotti, and Arin Murphy-Hiscock for feedback and encouragement along the way and for making the dream possible.

To the trailblazing, amazing, powerful women I have had the privilege to meet and learn from, including Olivia Robertson, Starhawk, Zsusanna Budapest, deTraci Regula, Susun Weed, and Ina May Gaskin.

To my cherished friends, Dr. Ann Gaba and Ruth Eichmiller, for their assistance with research materials, letting me borrow their computers when mine was down, and endless moral support. To the extraordinarily talented gentlemen of the tranceSenders, my band: Douglas Lichterman, Kenji Tajima, and Roland Auer. Thank you for keeping the mike on during my hiatus while writing, and special thanks to Douglas for backing me up in more ways than one.

To the inspiring, beautiful women whom I am honored to call my friends and whose magical influence is felt in these pages: Gretchen Greaser, Leigh Brown, Debby Schwartz, Shaula Chambliss, Dena Moes, Cayne Miceli, Misi Chavez, Samantha Franklin, Julie Gillis, Barbara Clark, Dawn Reed, Diane Saarinen, Iris Sierke, Llisa Jones-Arant, Deborah Merwyn, and the memory of Susan Sherill.

And to my little one, who at the time of this writing is still yet to be—thank you for inspiring me and for all those little kicks that remind me that I am never alone.

Introduction

Your spiritual journey begins with a shimmer of recognition; something new and strange that seems instantly familiar. Perhaps it is a memory from a past life, perhaps a glimmer of reality rising from the collective unconscious of all humanity. She comes to you in a dream, slowly and deliberately. You feel a sense of longing and desire. Something has been missing from your life, something you have desperately needed, something you cannot name. This presence speaks to your very soul. She is in the air that you breathe, the ground that you walk upon. She is the Divine Feminine. She has been asleep within you all these years.

Now, she is awakening and you cannot deny the strength of her presence. You seek to know her, to learn of her great mysteries, and to walk the path of those who honor her. You thirst for the knowledge of what came before, before our modern world became so unbalanced.

You have discovered the Goddess. She has found you. She has called out your name from the dark recesses of your mind. She has called you to herself. She is the source from which all of creation emanates. You feel amazed that she has been there all along but you have never known her name until now. She was called Isis by the Egyptians, Inanna by the Sumerians, Ishtar in Babylon. You know her. You are home.

Time passes. Seasons change. You discover your own psychic being. The Goddess guides you to explore your gifts. You develop your intuition and learn to trust it. You honor her and she blesses you with her bounty. You marvel at how she transforms your life in such perfect and subtle ways. Recognizing the power of change, you stand in awe at the turning of the seasons. You see the beauty in all creatures on earth. You seek to tread lightly upon the earth that is her body, knowing that all life comes from it and will one day ultimately return to it. You are becoming a witch.

You have taken your first steps on the path and are learning the Craft of the Wise. It begins with a longing and evolves into a tradition. You now have a name for things that were once purely instinctual. You discover that others share your beliefs. You are not alone. Her presence touches all aspects of

A Witch's Grimoire

your life in ways you could never express, although you are compelled to try. You know that others have gone before you and that the secrets of magic are yours to discover. You are evolving and becoming, your spirit transforming. You are undertaking a great journey, ever unfolding and ever changing.

Your newfound wisdom is inspiring. You want to share it. Your newfound wisdom is powerful and sometimes frightening. You want to keep it secret. You want to remember this place in time, this new beginning. You have been changed by her. You have even given yourself a new name. You want to hold on to this moment in time forever, never to forget how it feels to truly experience the divine presence in your life, to see how she works and moves and changes you.

You pick up a pen and begin to write. You are beginning your first book of shadows. You are creating your own personal grimoire.

1

Book of Memory

A grimoire is defined as a book of spells and incantations used for calling forth spirits. The word "grimoire" is related to the word "grammar," which pertains to the rules and the relationships of language. Derived from the Middle English *gramere* and the Old French *gramaire*, the root of the word is an alteration of the Latin *grammatica*, which we can trace back to its source from the Greek feminine of *grammatikos*, meaning "of letters." It seems appropriate that this feminine derivative from the language of one of the earliest classical pantheistic civilizations has evolved to describe what is now considered by many witches to be a sacred text devoted to rituals honoring the Mother Goddess. Most of the books that are now commonly classified as grimoires, however, were written during the Middle Ages and the Renaissance. They speak of many different traditions of ceremonial magic, both sacred and profane.

From Days of Old: What Is a Grimoire?

Most often, today's grimoire is handwritten by individuals for their own personal use. In a grimoire, there may be specific

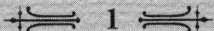

A Witch's Grimoire

instructions that pertain to a particular tradition, or it may contain strictly personal records intended only for the use of the individual author. Sometimes the grimoire (or sections of it) is passed down or copied from a master book. The term *grimoire* is generic and may be used in place of the title of the actual book, which is often kept secret.

What is popularly known as the "book of shadows" is really a sort of Wiccan recipe book that includes spells and incantations, but also much more. A book of shadows may also contain dreams, poems, invocations, revelations, inspiration, and lore.

Every grimoire is essentially a book of shadows, but not every book of shadows would conform to the definition of a grimoire. A book of shadows differs from a grimoire in that while it includes elements of the grimoire, it is not necessarily an exclusively instructive tome, but more of a personal record of a spiritual journey.

Some people argue that a book of shadows more closely resembles a diary or a journal and that highly personal musings have no place in the more didactic grimoire. Purists insist that the grimoire should be entirely instructional, full of information, annotation, and practical application. Fortunately for our purposes, there exists no officially designated criterion for creating a book of shadows, nor is there a correct or incorrect way of building, blessing, and using your personal grimoire.

In this book, we will begin the process of learning how to document the spiritual journey of one who follows the path of the Goddess. For our purposes, the grimoire and the book of shadows will henceforth be considered interchangeable and highly mutable: as unique and individual as the practitioner.

The most influential book of shadows is attributed to Gerald Gardner and Doreen Valiente. This highly regarded book was a compilation of inherited rituals that the authors blended and incorporated with original and modern elements. Their method is perhaps the most effective and traditional way of creating a book of shadows.

Book of Memory

You will take the knowledge that is the gift of our elders and ancestors and combine it with your own practices and beliefs to create a new, useful work that is rooted in your tradition but remains unique and original. This practice is entirely in line with the teachings of Wicca, which has no rigid forms but is fluid and changing, just like the seasons we celebrate. Just as every coven, or group of witches, is autonomous, so is each unique individual. It follows to reason that every book of shadows will in turn be the unique and definitive expression of the witch who wrote it.

The root of the word "witch" is derived from Wicca or *wicce*, the religious practice of worshipping both a goddess and a god as equal but opposite entities revered as the balanced essence of divinity. Although some claim that Wicca or *wicce* comes from the word "wise," others claim that its origin lies in the root of the idea "to shape or to bend." This is particularly interesting because it may well be said that the goal of magic is to bend or shape things to reflect our will. Certainly, wisdom would be a necessity for an individual interested in practicing magic to shape or change a given circumstance or condition!

The "power" in Wicca is bestowed upon us by the Goddess that we may do good works in the world such that all beings may benefit. It is by no means an implication of power over any other person. Thus it is with the understanding that true power comes from the divine and is never used to dominate or otherwise subordinate the will of another that you begin the process of creating your grimoire, the physical manifestation of your spiritual journey. Writing the story of your spiritual awakening and subsequent journey can be a very empowering method of self-discovery. You will be able to make connections between divine power (which manifests by the grace of the Goddess) and personal power (which radiates from within). You will recognize writing as a ritual in itself, creating a sacred tool that contains the chronicle of the magic that will unfold.

As you write, you will chart your path and look back to see your growth. You will learn and change and you may become passionate about keeping the records of your spiritual and psychic progress. You will create word magic where before there were only blank pages. You will forge new traditions based on ancient rites. You will keep this as a gift to yourself, to be shared only as you will it so. You will rekindle the archetypal knowledge that has been so diluted by the trappings of our modern consciousness. You will rediscover the seasons, you will honor the passing of time, and you will celebrate life, death, and rebirth—each account recorded in your own hand.

The Journey Begins: Why Should You Write a Grimoire?

You have chosen a unique and, at times, difficult path. Worshipping the Goddess and the God, while it is by no means a new phenomenon, is certainly unusual in our modern society. When one thinks of the world's religions today, Christianity, Judaism, Islam, Hinduism, and Buddhism immediately come to mind. Wicca as a religion barely registers in mainstream consciousness. Although we have seen a great re-emergence in the acknowledgment of the Divine Feminine in recent years, by no means have the scales been balanced. We can walk through the halls of museums and find numerous statues of gods or God and the saints. But the Goddess is usually tucked away, around a dark corner, nearly hidden at the end of a corridor, even though some of the ancient figures suggest that Goddess worship may date back as far as 30,000 years ago. While for many, this information might be an earth-shattering revelation, exploding the myths, beliefs, and practices that have forbidden women from attaining priesthood or having direct communion with the divine, the Goddess is often treated as an archaeological afterthought. Images of goddesses are relegated to being mere curiosities, fertility amulets and fetishes and dolls. They have lost their broader meaning and religious stature.

By writing your story, you are taking responsibility for the idea that the clearest pathway to the Goddess is through direct experience. In writing

Book of Memory

your story, you are preserving the intimate details of divine communion. Initiation is something that a witch achieves; it is not necessarily bestowed upon an individual by another person. True awakening comes most often directly from the Goddess. While we may enact rituals to celebrate and acknowledge such a transition, no one of us can detect the exact moment when an initiation occurs for someone else. That is between the deity and the devotee.

A grimoire can thus be much more than just a personal record. While it is inspired by those who have gone before, it also can serve as a guide for those just discovering the Wiccan path. It can remind us of where we came from and how far we still have to go. We can revisit our steps and learn anew. We can learn of our sacred origin when we reflect upon our own spiritual beginnings. The grimoire is the gateway to our minds. It is a sacred tool and should always be treated as such.

Carved in Stone: Where Does the Grimoire Come From?

Since early civilizations first invented it, writing has evolved into a necessary communication tool. However, the act and learning of writing was once a privilege and not accessible to all. Since Wicca is based on pre-Christian religion, it seems only appropriate that we look at the ancient writings that recognize the female aspect of deity to consider the roots and origins of the grimoire.

It can be said that the Sumerian cuneiform tablets of Inanna could well be considered the very first grimoire. Inanna, the Queen of Heaven and Earth, is the first named goddess in recorded history. She was also known as the First Daughter of the Moon and the Morning and Evening Star. Her worship dates back to ancient Sumer, some 2,000 years before Christ. The story of Inanna is the story of life, death, and rebirth. She is the source of life that brings forth creation. She descends into the underworld to face

A Witch's Grimoire

her sister, the dark goddess, Ereshkigal. She rises from the underworld to reclaim her throne. She discovers upon returning that her beloved consort, Dimuzi, has usurped her throne. She loves, she suffers for love, and her glory is ultimately restored. Her legends and songs were inscribed in cuneiform on 5,000 to 6,000 clay tablets, which now reside in museums spread across the world. In these tablets are love stories, songs of lament, lessons, and myths. Without the work of diligent scholars from many parts of the world, this forgotten liturgy of a religion from long ago would be lost.

It is interesting to note that, centuries later, across Mesopotamia in Babylon, a very similar mythology was created. The Babylonians worshipped Ishtar, the King Maker, Lady of Victory, Queen of Heaven. Ishtar is a sister goddess to Inanna in that her story also depicts the lost love of a youth. Her lover, Tammuz, is slain by a wild boar. After his death, Ishtar journeys to the underworld to reclaim her love. During her journey, she must pass through seven gates. At each gate, she sacrifices a symbol of her divinity. She lays aside her crown, all of her sacred adornments, and finally, her veil. When Ishtar sacrifices her veil, she forgets who she is, she forgets that she is a goddess, and she grovels in the decay of the underworld. When she finds Tammuz in the underworld, she does not recognize him, nor does he recognize her. What they do recognize, however, is their love for each other, and through the realization that love transcends identity and even life itself, death is conquered, the goddess is restored, and life on earth is also reborn in full abundance. The myths of this goddess journeyed throughout the centuries across many lands.

Hieroglyphs on papyrus scrolls and clay tablets from the twenty-first dynasty of Egypt tell the story of Isis and Osiris. According to myth, Isis and Osiris are sister and brother twins who fall in love with each other within their mother's womb. As husband and wife, they are inseparable until Osiris is overthrown by their brother, Set. Set builds an elaborate sarcophagus in the likeness of Osiris and persuades him to lie down inside it. Once Osiris is inside, Set slams the lid closed and seals Osiris inside, presumably

Book of Memory

to his death. Set then hides the sarcophagus containing the body of Osiris inside a tamarisk tree.

As Isis searches for him, she finds the tree, which is hidden within a pillar of the royal house of the city of Byblos. To gain access to the queen, Isis, in disguise, befriends her handmaidens. The queen is enchanted with Isis and employs her as a nursemaid to her son. At night, Isis transforms herself into a swallow and flies around the pillar, singing her lament. She also loves the child and attempts to give him the gift of immortality by bathing his body in flames every night, but one night, the queen discovers Isis holding the infant in the hearth and becomes hysterical. Isis sweeps the baby into her arms, unharmed, and furiously reveals her true nature to the bewildered queen. Confronted with the power of the goddess and seeing that their son is unharmed, the king and queen make the connection between Isis in mourning and the swallow that circles the pillar, and the king gives the pillar to Isis. It is through the power of the goddess that Osiris is resurrected.

Isis and Osiris embody the essence of the polarity of deity, female and male, symbiotic yet opposite entities, each irrevocably connected to the other. Of the two, Isis is dominant and considered to be more powerful. She was the lawgiver of ancient Egypt, known as the Mother of all Creation. Their story is one of transformation. Her enchantment and power was enacted in pageants and rituals across the land and her worship reached as far away as Rome and even the British Isles. Her image appears in carvings, statues, and jewelry from 1000 B.C.E. to 400 C.E.

Without the records of stories such as these, preserved for thousands of years, it would be difficult—if not impossible—to piece together the rites of worship dedicated to the powerful and far-reaching Goddess.

VOICES FROM THE PAST

The religious practices upon which Wicca is partially based were primarily an oral tradition passed down to neophytes by more experienced practitioners. It's said that small groups of practitioners met in secret and would possess little knowledge of the whereabouts or practices of other groups. This was done for protection, so that if one group was discovered there would be no way for the members to reveal or disclose the whereabouts of other practitioners. Unfortunately, this fragmented approach has left us severely wanting in the area of verifiable information. It is very difficult to piece together the rites and rituals of an oral tradition when the practitioners are scattered and disjointed and few written records exist. Consider this excerpt from the Preface to the *Book of Shadows* as recorded by Doreen Valiente, who adapted selected works of Gerald Gardner, considered by many to be the father of modern Wicca:

> *Keep a book in your own hand of write. Let brothers and sisters copy what they will; but never let the book out of your hands and never keep the writings of another, for if found in their hand of write they may well be taken and tortured. Each shall guard his own writing and destroy it whenever danger threatens. Learn as much as you may by heart, and when danger is past, rewrite your book if it be safe. For this reason, if any die, destroy their book if they have not been able to for an' it be found 'tis clear proof against them, and "ye may not be a witch alone," so all their friends be in danger of torture. So destroy everything not necessary. If your book be found on you 'tis clear proof against you alone and you may be tortured. Keep all thoughts of the cult from your mind an' say you had bad dreams, a devil caused you to write this without your knowledge. Think to yourself, "I know nothing. I remember nothing. I have forgotten all." Drive this into your mind . . .*

While this preface has never been proven to be authentic, it is certainly a fascinating representation of the threat of capture that many witches experienced.

When so much information is missing, it becomes our responsibility to rewrite the rituals and legends as they relate to our modern experience. We may never go back, only forward.

Book of Memory

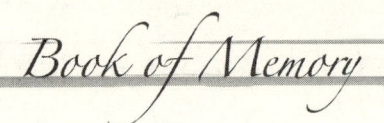

Begin at the Beginning: Choose Your Book

There are many traditions of Wicca including Gardnerian, Alexandrian, Saxon, Dianic, Welsh, Irish, and general Celtic. There are also many self-invented witches who do not subscribe to any specific tradition other than the ones they adapt and create. They often refer to themselves as Eclectics.

Your grimoire need not be elaborate, but it certainly can be if that reflects your personality and if you consider your practice formal or ceremonial in nature. The type of book that you choose to consecrate as your grimoire should be a reflection of who you are. For some, a spiral-bound notebook or a three-ring binder will do just fine.

Although we will be focusing on the content of the grimoire rather than the book itself, it should be noted that there are myriad choices available. We only need to walk into the local bookshop and investigate the blank journal section to find an appropriate book. Most art supply stores will contain basic black sketchbooks of various sizes with fine grade white, unlined paper. Artisans will also create and sell handmade books complete with handmade paper and leather embossed covers.

Decide what kind of book inspires you. Some questions to help you make your decision include the following:

- Will you want to carry the book around with you at all times?
- Will you consider the writing in your grimoire to be a private ritual, only to be done as part of or after a magical rite?
- Will the book reside on your altar or in your backpack? Does it need to be portable?
- Do you want it to lock so its contents are secure from prying, curious eyes?
- Would you consider making the book yourself?

These are things to reflect on before making a decision about what type of book you will be most inspired by, that you will enjoy writing in, that you will consider a magical tool in its own right.

If you are the artistic and crafty type, as many witches are, you may find that making your own book is a rewarding project, for then you will truly have a one-of-a-kind grimoire, one unlike any other, imbued with your own personal energy. Making a book from recycled items is not as difficult as you may think and it is certainly in line with the ecologically minded tenets of Wicca. While it may be a messy endeavor, it can be very gratifying as well. Even if creating the entire book seems to be a daunting and time-consuming enterprise, consider creating just a few handmade pages for special incantations and spells to add to your book. Whether you buy your book in a store or make it at home, you can add herbs and flowers to customize and personalize the pages.

Craft Your Own: Make the Grimoire from Scratch

The art of papermaking has its origins in China and ancient Egypt. Practitioners who resonate strongly with Kwan Yin or Isis may feel particularly inspired by this choice. Making your own paper from recycled items does not require any specialized equipment. It is a lovely ecological expression and a very attractive one. You will only need simple household items, many of which you may already possess. As we have already learned from those who have gone before, everyday household items can be instruments of potent magic indeed!

Homemade Paper for Your Grimoire

The basis of a handmade paper is pulp. You can make pulp from almost any kind of paper, but avoid using any paper with a glossy surface, such as pages out of magazines. These are treated with chemicals and unsuitable for the purpose of recycled papermaking. Remember, just because something is recycled, this in no way has any adverse affect on the quality.

Materials Needed
- Paper, such as tissue, computer paper, writing or typing paper, paper bags
- A bucket
- Cold, clean water (add a few drops of Florida water or rose water)
- Two wooden frames; these can be picture frames, but the corners must be tight and secured
- A piece of mesh (net curtaining or window screen) to fit in frames; the finer the mesh, the smoother the paper
- Staples
- Blender
- Tablespoon or ladle
- Large plastic bowl (big enough to easily accommodate the frames)
- Liquid laundry starch
- Optional: dried or fresh flowers, leaves, or bits of lace; food coloring or dyes suitable for cotton fabrics; anything for added color that pleases you
- Palette knife or butter knife
- Athame
- Absorbent cloths, such dish towels or Handi-Wipes (one for each page of paper you intend to make)
- Heavy book, chopping block, or brick

- Optional: A pentacle, an ankh, an eight-pointed star, or an amulet that you normally wear on your person, to be used as an embossing tool

1. Tear the paper into postage stamp-size pieces and soak the pieces overnight in a plastic bucket of cold, clean water. You can make this first step into a magical practice by adding a few drops of Florida water or rose water to the water in the bucket and by asking the Goddess to bless your work. As you tear the paper into bits, focus your energy into the paper and make your intentions known by reciting the following: "Goddess, bless this endeavor of art. By my hand, let the transformation begin so that your presence be known in the world for the benefit of all. So mote it be."

2. Stretch the mesh over one of the frames and staple it so that it's very taut. This covered frame will be used to pick up the pulp and keep it flat. If the mesh is loose, the paper will be saggy and difficult to remove from the frame. The empty frame will be held on top of the mesh frame and will give your paper a nice edge. Set the frames aside until step 6.

3. After your paper has soaked overnight, pour off the excess water and begin transferring the pulp into a blender, spoonful by spoonful.

4. Add water until the pitcher of the blender is no more than three-quarters full. Run the blender for about fifteen seconds, and then check the pulp to make sure it is broken down evenly. If necessary, stir the pulp and then run the blender for another five seconds.

5. Gently pour the pulp into the plastic bowl. At this point, you can add a spoonful of liquid laundry starch to the pulp. This

Book of Memory

will make your paper absorb the ink better, so there will be less of a tendency for the ink to bleed when you are writing.

6. Stir the pulp gently and wait for the movement of the water to cease. At the moment when the water is still—but the pulp has not yet settled—hold the frames securely in your hands with the empty frame on top and the mesh frame with the mesh facing up directly underneath it. Slide the frames under the water in a smooth motion, scooping up a layer of pulp. It may take some practice to get the pulp evenly distributed over the mesh frame.

7. Keeping the frames steady and flat, lift them out of the water and allow the water to drain away. A layer of pulp should cover the mesh screen. Remove the empty frame.

8. Consider pressing herbs and flowers into the wet surface. Thinking about using this paper for a protection spell? Why not use a sprig of rosemary along the edges? Perhaps you have a love spell in mind. Adorn some of your pages with red rose petals. You can set aside the pages decorated with flowers and herbs for specific use within your grimoire. Use whatever your mind is inspired to create. Do you feel a special connection to the goddess Ariadne? Include some silken threads. Enchanted by faerie glamour? Sprinkle some glitter across the paper. Make it your own.

9. Carefully remove the paper from the frame while it is still wet. A palette knife or butter knife will be a useful tool for loosening the edges, or if you wish you can use your athame, consecrating each page as you make it.

A Witch's Grimoire

10. Once you have removed the paper, lay it carefully on one half of the absorbent cloth and, without folding your page, fold the other half of the cloth over the paper to absorb the excess water. Continue stacking individual pages in this fashion, making sure layers of cloth alternate with sheets of paper.

11. Put something waterproof (like plastic wrap) at the top of the stack of paper, then place a heavy book or chopping block on the top. This will weigh the paper down and keep it flat while drying.

12. You can add magical energy to your paper by embossing magical symbols in it. Embossed paper is made by pressing an object into the paper while the paper is still wet, then removing the object. If you want a well-defined motif, leave the embossing tool there as the paper is weighted and do not remove it until the paper is completely dry.

Feel free to experiment. The more energy you put into creating your book of shadows, the more you will enjoy using it.

Bind Your Grimoire

Whether or not you have gone to the trouble of making your own paper, you can still make your own book by assembling blank pages and binding your book. If you have chosen the 100 percent homemade route, these next few steps will give you some finishing options. These are meant to inspire you as you complete the construction of your book of shadows by selecting a cover and then binding the book together.

Materials Needed for Cover and Spine
- Binding board or heavier stock paper from a craft store; you can wrap the cover in cloth, securing the cloth with good PVA glue (see end of material list)
- Scissors
- Ruler
- Scoring tool
- Binder clips or similar clamps
- Heavy book, chopping block, or brick
- If you are planning on using glue to bind, use a heavy brush and PVA (polyvinyl acetate or adhesive) glue, which is the most durable. If you want to avoid chemicals, use another more natural type of paste or glue.
- If you'd rather not use glue to bind, use a cord or ribbon (red or your favorite color). You'll need a drill or hole punch and a template for placing the holes. Mark them with a pencil.

1. Decide on the material for your cover.

2. Cut two equal-size pieces that are slightly larger than the pages of the book.

A Witch's Grimoire

3. Measure about one-quarter inch from the edge of each piece and score lightly so your book will open and close easily.

4. Set aside a strip of the cover material or an extra sheet of paper to use for covering the spine.

5. Assemble all of your pages and front and back covers in a stack and clamp them together firmly with binder clips or clamps. It is very important to stack the pages very neatly, for they will be permanently assembled in the configuration you have them in now. Any adjusting should be done at this point or you will have crooked pages in your book. Also, put small pieces of wood under the clamps so you do not have clamp marks on your cover.

6. Line up the pages so that the edge of the stack is hanging slightly over the edge of the table you are working on. This edge will become the spine of the book.

7. Use a heavy book or a brick to weigh down the pages and keep them still.

Note: If you are not going to use glue to make the spine, skip to step 12 for instructions on binding with ribbon.

8. With a brush, spread glue very thickly all along the edges of the pages at the spine. Allow sufficient time for the glue to dry thoroughly.

9. The spine should be the same length as the cover of your book and three times the thickness of the book. You can determine the thickness of your book by measuring the total height of the

Book of Memory

stacked pages. Multiply this number by three, and you will get the correct width of the spine. Draw two parallel lines with a pencil on the inside of the spine (the side you intend to glue onto the book so the pencil marks will not show), dividing the spine into three equal parts. These lines will be your scoring guide.

10. Score the cover material along the edge of a metal ruler with your scoring tool. Be careful not to cut through the spine; just score it deep enough so that it can be easily folded.

11. Glue the strip along the edge of the book so that the previously glued area is completely hidden. Allow the spine cover to dry, and your book is bound.

12. If you prefer to try another binding technique, you can use cord or ribbon. This method does not require a spine. After the pages are clamped, punch or drill holes along one side of your book. If you are using a hole punch, first make a template so all the holes will be the same distance from the left edge of the pages. Do not attempt to punch holes through the template, but use the template to mark in pencil where the holes should be on each page, and then punch them out individually. This will make the holes more accurate, and your finished book will be more attractive.

If power tools are your thing, you can drill very slowly through the clamped stack and achieve the same result in less time. Be sure your pages are securely clamped together so that none of them slip while you're drilling.

13. Use a ribbon or cord that is five times the length of your book. You can use a red cord to symbolize your connection to the Great Mother or your favorite color, or any other ribbon, cord, or sturdy thread that pleases you. Push the ribbon through the first hole at the top of the book, leaving a tail of two inches or more.

14. With the tail in place, weave the ribbon through all the remaining holes. When you reach the end, wrap the ribbon around the bottom and go back again through the hole you just used. Continue weaving the ribbon back through the holes up to the top, envisioning the spiral dance of the Goddess as you go.

15. Once the ribbon is through the last hole, wrap it tight around the top, as you did at the bottom, and tie it together with the tail end.

Consecrate Your Grimoire: As It Is Written, Let It Be Done

With the construction of your magical grimoire now complete, it is time to dedicate your book to its sacred purpose. This charm will work well whether your grimoire is handmade or not. The most important thing is to endow it with your strong intention to do good works in the world and to record them so that they may be of benefit to all beings.

1. Light a yellow candle and call upon Sophia, embodiment of holy wisdom, to guide you.

2. Burn frankincense upon your altar.

3. Hold the book slightly opened over the rising smoke, allowing it to drift through the pages.

Book of Memory

4. Turn the pages slowly and gently, letting the sacred smoke waft throughout your new book of shadows. Speak the following words, or improvise your own:

Blessed be this instrument of art, By my hand (or human hands) you were made,
By magic, be now changed!
No more an ordinary book in my eyes
But a grimoire dedicated to the Craft of the Wise.
By all the power of three times three,
As I will, so mote it be.

5. Hold the book on your right hand and place your left hand on top of the book and imagine all of the changes and lessons yet to come.

6. Imagine all the witches you know of and admire, both contemporary and historical, all those who are older and younger than you. Picture yourself in the middle of a growing circle. To your left are those who are older. To your right are those who are younger. To the left of the elders are those who have passed on. Picture the circle growing as you imagine the lives of all witches who have gone before you. To the right of those who are younger, imagine the cycle of life continuing, extending outward to encompass all of those yet to be born.

7. Recognize your place in the spiral of time and this task that you have chosen. See yourself within the context of humanity and companionship. When the image is clear in your mind, speak these words aloud:

Wisdom of the ages
Be with me here now.
Sacred book of changes

A Witch's Grimoire

This promise I vow:
To honor those who have gone before
To preserve the secrets, legends, and lore
To hold my place in the spiral of time
Contained within my sacred grimoire.

Harvest Your Records

Now that you have created and dedicated your grimoire, it is time to start gathering records to put in it. You will want to include many things specific to your own tradition, but you will also want to generate new ideas and record information that is specific to your own direct experience. Take some time to think about the book blessing you just performed.

[?] Did you experience a change in the energy surrounding you? How does your book of shadows seem to you now that you have dedicated it to a sacred purpose? Perhaps you have dedicated your spiritual work to a particular aspect of the Goddess. You may wish to invoke her at the beginning. Use this space to write down ideas for your own personal book blessing.

_____

_____

_____

_____

_____

Book of Memory

Once you have worked out some ideas that you are pleased and comfortable with, it is time to start thinking about the individual pages and the organization of the book. The first page can be a dedicatory page, stating your magical name or craft name, the date on which you began writing in this book, the deity to whom you are devoted, and any insignias or symbols you wish to include.

In the tradition of secrecy, many witches opt to write in a mystical script used for ceremonial magic. The very name "book of shadows" refers to that which is hidden in mystery. In case a book of shadows was discovered by an inappropriate person or if it somehow fell into the wrong hands, the person making the discovery would be unable to read its contents, unless of course they were well versed in the Theban Alphabet or adept with runes. And if the person were not a witch, this would probably not be the case. You can explore the option of writing only certain parts of the book in runes if you want it to be accessible to others. Following are some examples of ceremonial alphabets you may use.

THE THEBAN ALPHABET

Although we cannot say for certain what the origins of the Theban Alphabet are, it is one of the most beautiful and widely used of the magical alphabets. Also referred to as the Witch's Alphabet or the Runes of Honorius, this ceremonial text came into use during the medieval period. It is believed Honorius of Thebes created this alphabet. This claim is attributed to the first known appearance of the Theban Alphabet, which was in Book III of the *Three Books of Occult Philosophy* by Cornelius Agrippa. Agrippa, published in Latin in 1533, attributes the preservation of the Theban Alphabet to the Italian writer and magician Petrus de Apono, who lived during the thirteenth century.

A Witch's Grimoire

THE FUTHARK RUNES

Often called the Older Rune Row, the Futhark Runes were first used by Germanic ceremonial magicians for divination, inspiration, and in inscriptions for magical workings. Although they do have phonetic correlations, the Furthark Runes never evolved into a spoken language. The name *futhark* is derived from the first six characters that appear in this system. According to Nordic legend, the runes were first spied by the god Odin as he hung from the Yggdrassil tree for nine days and nights. The runes are also considered an oracle, with each individual rune containing a specific esoteric message.

Book of Memory

Number	Shape	Phonetic Value	Name
1	ᚠ	F	fehu
2	ᚢ	U	uruz
3	ᚦ	TH	thurisaz
4	ᚨ	A	ansuz
5	ᚱ	R	raidho
6	ᚲ	K	kaunaz
7	ᚷ	G	gebo
8	ᚹ	W	wunjo
9	ᚺ	H	hagalaz
10	ᚾ	N	nauthiz
11	ᛁ	I	isa
12	ᛃ	J	jera
13	ᛇ	EI	eihaw
14	ᛈ	P	perthro
15	ᛉ	Z	elhaz
16	ᛋ	S	sowilo
17	ᛏ	T	teiwaz
18	ᛒ	B	berkano
19	ᛖ	E	ehwaz
20	ᛗ	M	mannaz
21	ᛚ	L	laguz
22	ᛜ	NG	ingwaz
23	ᛞ	D	dagaz
24	ᛟ	O	othala

THE FAERIE RUNES

The Faerie Runes are derived from the Saxon art of invoking faeries. The Saxon priestesses claim that those who seek communion with the faerie realm must use these runes, as they are the only runes that these ethereal

A Witch's Grimoire

creatures will respond to. While the Faerie Runes are believed to have originated in North Umbria around the year 1463, they have been passed down through the lineage of priestesses of Wessex. The runes are meant to be carved on magical tools dedicated to summoning faeries. The names of the faeries one wishes to call upon must only be written in these runes.

A:	B:	C:	D:
E:	F:	G:	H:
I:	J:	K:	L:
M:	N:	O:	P:
Q:	R:	S:	T:
U:	V:	W:	X:
	Y:	Z:	

2

Book of Foundation

With your consecrated grimoire in place, it is now time to start thinking about the context in which you will write. You will want your writing to be inspired by magic and ritual. How you move and act in your ritual space will have a direct impact on how you interact with the spiritual plane. It is important to prepare your body and your mind, for they are irrevocably connected to your spirit, at least in this life.

Because of the nature of Wicca, there are very few recognized centers where one may practice this religion. Many covens meet in members' homes or on their private property. Even if you have a coven that you regularly meet with, you will still need to define your magical space within the context of your own home. You will be using your book of shadows to record not only spells and lore, but also your dreams and visions.

Most Wiccans and witches have at least one altar in their home. An altar is more than just an artfully arranged collection of curious objects. It represents the fundamental nature of devotion on the material plane. It is with our magical tools that we seek to uncover the hidden mysteries of the Goddess. Like the book of shadows, the altar is also physical representation of our relationship with deity.

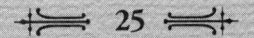

Steps on the Wiccan Path

Begin your ritual preparation by making a conscious decision to enter the time and space we refer to as "between the worlds." Turn off your computer. Unplug your telephone. Dim the lights. Light a candle or two or three. Do not let your mind be intruded upon by the outside world. Seek to open yourself up to benevolent influences that extend far beyond the reach of our mundane world. Relax and breathe. Clear your mind. One by one, begin to release your distractions, letting them flow farther and farther away from you. Sit on the floor facing your altar.

Were you subjected to a demanding boss or difficult customers for most of the day? Picture this person or these people in front of you. Focus on their image for a moment and imagine the image growing transparent until it completely disintegrates and vanishes into the ether.

Tired of answering an incessantly ringing phone? Allow yourself to hear the tones one last time, as they grow softer and softer and farther and farther away until they are completely inaudible.

Exhausted from performing physical labor? Close your eyes and breathe deeply. Accept the fact that for this day, your work is done. Drop your shoulders, leave the working hours in the past, and allow the physical strain to depart.

Concerned about finances? Focus on the bounty of the Goddess and realize that whatever you have at this time is enough.

Preoccupied with the problems, stresses, and the concerns of others? Let the anxiety fall away.

Sit with your spine straight and breathe deeply. Picture a radiant ball of energy located in the center of your being, your solar plexus, just below your chest and above your navel. As you continue to breathe, allow the light to grow. As you inhale, understand that you are taking into your body the surrounding air, transforming it into energy. As you exhale, your cares are released. Get in touch with this cycle of breathing, of energy released and replenished, replenished and released.

Book of Foundation

Touch the floor with the palms of your hands as you breathe in, imagining that you are gathering energy from the earth beneath you, beneath your home. Picture the earth. Now send your energy outward so that you can psychically touch things beyond your physical reach. Your reach extends beyond the floorboards, beyond the foundations of your home, deep into the sacred earth.

Call up the energy as you breathe in. Let it flow through you, and as you exhale, send it spiraling into your center, transforming into a glowing light that you hold within the core of your being. When this image becomes very clear, visualize the glowing ball of energy moving slightly, first spiraling within itself, and then traveling up and down a bit. Realize that as you breathe, you are taking in energy from the air and transforming it into living breath. You are also taking in energy from the earth and transforming it into active power.

Stay focused and let the rising ball of energy reach your heart. Experience this as an embrace from the Goddess, the power of the earth moving through you according to your will. Envision the ball of energy separating and becoming two distinct spheres. As the spheres separate, they travel to your shoulders. Feel the warmth surrounding your shoulders as you would if you were walking in the bright daylight, even though your room or temple space is dim.

Let the spheres of pulsing, glowing light travel slowly down your arms, experiencing each movement as a distinct sensation. Your shoulders drop and are more relaxed. Any residual tension in your arms completely dissipates. Your wrists are limp. You are surrendering to the beauty of this power, even as you are directing it. The energy fills your hands and permeates even to your fingertips.

Turn your hands over so that your palms are facing up. Slowly raise your arms. Imagine sending this energy outward to touch all beings. Extend your arms with your palms facing outward in an invoking gesture. Breathe deeply and feel how this transforming energy changes you.

A Witch's Grimoire

Open your eyes and look around the room. Notice how your perception has changed. Lower your arms slowly and let your hands touch the floor once again. Continue focusing on the cycle of breath, releasing and replenishing energy. As you exhale, send the energy back into the earth from whence it came. Breathe deeply.

You should feel relaxed, but not the least bit sleepy. Tranquil, but invigorated and alive, in touch with the earth and with the delicate energies to which the intuitive mind is open. Think about how a simple act such as grounding your energy and opening your psychic center can heighten your awareness.

Any place where you practice magic is your temple. At the center of the temple is the priestess. Prepare yourself to meet your destiny. Remember your sacred origin. Use the following space to write down your memories of how you came to choose the Wiccan path. If your spiritual awakening was recent, this should be easy. If you have been a practicing witch for some time, get to know yourself all over again.

[?] Remember how it was in the beginning, where you lived, if you practiced solitary or with others. Who were they? Who were you at that time in your life?

_____

_____

_____

_____

_____

Book of Foundation

Create Sacred Space

Once you have mastered the techniques of grounding and centering your energy through repetition, you are ready to transfer this energy into your surrounding environment. Creating sacred space is just as important as preparing yourself for magical workings. You are, in essence, raising a temple for meditation, worship, divination, spell casting, or whatever aspect of the Craft you are called upon by the Goddess to enact. There are many ways to dedicate a sacred space. You can begin by anointing each corner of the room with oil, creating an equal-armed cross contained within a circle. This represents the balance of female and male energies, circle of creation, the four directions, and the four elements.

Next, take a broom and sweep the room thoroughly, concentrating on not only removing actual dust, but also psychically removing any unwanted energies or influences. Any action that is accompanied by a strong and specific intention becomes a ritual. If you sweep the room with your only intention being to clear away the dust, then that is all that will happen. But if you focus with clear intent on removing old, unwanted energies, you will most likely be successful in doing so.

After your initial, vigorous physical sweeping is done, focus on a different type of cleansing, a cleansing of the ethereal space. Begin in the east and work your way clockwise around the room, drawing a circle. Sweep in the air, just above the floor. When you have gone around your circle three times, lay the broom on the floor inside the circle and visualize all of the negative energy sinking into the earth and dissolving. Let it be broken down by the roots of trees and plants to be transformed again in the great cauldron of the dark mother.

Make Your Own Incense

You can further cleanse the space by burning incense. Because you can never be absolutely certain of its contents or of its quality, it is not advisable to use just any type of joss stick incense. Instead, you can make your own incense—it is inexpensive and much more effective. A resin-based incense does not contain any combustibles, and will not ignite and burn on its own. A charcoal must be used. Though this is relatively safe for indoor use, a piece of charcoal can produce a great amount of heat and must be handled with care.

Materials Needed
- Mortar and pestle
- Your cauldron, a heat-resistant ceramic dish, or a shell placed on a trivet, to prevent any damage to the surface your incense container is resting upon
- Two resins
- Small charcoal briquette (available in metaphysical shops)
- Matches or a lighter

1. Combine two resins, such as equal amounts of copal and frankincense, in your mortar and pestle. Crush them thoroughly until they become a fine powder.

2. Light a small piece of charcoal and place it in the cauldron (or shell or other vessel). Allow the charcoal to glow red before adding your incense.

3. Add the powder slowly, just a pinch at a time, allowing each pinch to burn completely before adding any more. This type of incense burning is slow and deliberate, with cleansing the residual energies in mind. If you dump all of the incense on the coal at once,

you will get an undesirable amount of smoke in the air at one time. The incense will burn very quickly and will not burn long enough to do its job effectively. Let the incense burn a little at a time until the coal is spent. With every pinch, recite the following incantation:

My mind is awake
My spirit, aware
At once now purified
Through this fire and air.

This brings us to the next level of cleansing. You will need two chalices or tall glasses. One will be filled with spring (or bottled) water. It is very important that the source of the water be kinetic and not static, for it is the essence of running water that gives this rite its potency. In the other chalice, place four pinches of salt, one for each direction.

1. Hold the chalice of water in your left hand and the chalice of salt in your right.

2. Pour the water into the chalice of salt, combining the two elements of water and earth.

3. Pour the now salted water back into the left chalice, dissolving the salt crystals so that the two distinct elements are thoroughly mixed. Continue pouring the water back and forth from hand-to-hand, repeating your intention:

With salt I purify
With water I cleanse
All things in accord
From beginning to end.

The purpose of consecrating a sacred space is to give yourself a dedicated realm in which to perform magic and ritual. This place is the material representation of "between the worlds," where devotees interact with deity. The altar becomes the table that humankind shares with the Goddess and the God.

Cast the Circle Thrice About

Once the space is consecrated, it is often desirable to cast a circle about the surrounding perimeter. This circle functions as a shield against any undesirable influences, as well as a container for the magical energy generated during rituals. One method of drawing the circle is performed by using a ceremonial sword, delineating the outer edge of the circle by tracing the point of the sword on the ground, and then by walking clockwise three times around the circle, beginning in the north or the east, as your personal practice or tradition recommends, accompanied by the following chant:

> *Thrice around the circle bound*
> *Evil sink into the ground.*
> *This charge I lay by the number three*
> *As my will, so mote it be.*

When doing rituals with a group, once the circle is cast, it is very important that no one leaves or enters it until it is opened. If it becomes absolutely necessary to admit or dismiss someone, use your athame to "cut" an opening in the circle so that the person can enter or depart. Use the blade to seal the opening once again.

When we work in a circle, we call upon the elemental powers of the four directions to witness our work.

Book of Foundation

INVOCATION TO THE EAST

Begin in the east, the land of new beginnings. The east is the realm of the dawn; its season is springtime. The east represents possibility and awareness. Look to the east when you seek to renew hope and faith, when you seek clarity of vision. The corresponding element to the east is air, and we invoke these powers by facing the east. Call the powers of this direction with this charge:

I call upon the spirits of air who guard and protect the gateway to the eastern realm, I beckon and call you forth from the far corner of the universe wherein you dwell. Winds of change, strength of tornadoes, bear witness to this rite and give us your aid! Gentle breeze that carries the seed to fertile soil, descend into this temple and grant us your blessing. Realm of the Dawning Star, land of sunrise and of springtime, bestow upon us your gifts of inspiration and song. We seek to know thee, we seek to honor thee. By the air that is our breath, we charge thee, be here now! To the East and the spirits of air, we bid thee hail and welcome!

INVOCATION TO THE SOUTH

Proceed around the circle and look to the south to face the direction of noontime and of summer. Turn to the south when you seek fulfillment of desire, when passion and inspiration are your needs. Face the south and call the powers of the direction with this charge:

I call upon the spirits of fire who guard and protect the gateway to the southern realm, I beckon and call you forth from the far corner of the universe wherein you dwell. Candle flame and hearth fire, come into this circle and lend warmth to our hearts. Strength of wildfire and volcano, descend into this temple and grant us your blessing. Brilliant orb of the high noon heat, realm of the risen sun, bestow upon us your gifts of fiery passion and inspiration. By the fire in our hearts, we charge thee, be here now! To the South and the spirits of fire, we bid thee hail and welcome!

INVOCATION TO THE WEST

Continue around the circle to the western "corner" and face the direction of sunset and of autumn. Turn to the west when you seek to enhance your intuition, uncover mysteries, and balance your emotions. Face the west and call the powers of the direction with this charge:

I call upon the spirits of water who guard and protect the gateway to the western realm, I beckon and call you forth from the far corner of the universe wherein you dwell. Ocean depths, cradle of life, come into this circle and show the truth of our visions. Strength of storm and tides, descend into this temple and grant us your blessing. Gentle rain that nourishes and cleanses, realm of the setting sun, bestow upon us your gifts of intuition and mystery. By the water in our blood, we charge thee, be here now! To the West and the spirits of water, we bid thee hail and welcome!

INVOCATION TO THE NORTH

Finally, you come to the north, the powers of elemental earth, representing both the womb and the grave, the source of all life and the ultimate end that awaits at the end of life. North is the season of winter and of midnight. Turn to the north when you wish to manifest outcomes and reveal truth. Face the north and call the powers of the direction with this charge:

Book of Foundation

I call upon the spirits of earth who guard and protect the gateway to the northern realm, I beckon and call you forth from the far corner of the universe wherein you dwell. Gaia, Demeter, Earth Mother, come into this circle and manifest the power of your divine law. Strength of earthquake and of mountain, descend into this temple and grant us your blessing. North Star, navigator's star, that which calls all other directions unto itself, realm of winter and of midnight, bestow upon us your gifts of strength. By the earth that is our body, we charge thee, be here now! To the North and the spirits of earth, we bid thee hail and welcome!

Craft Your Invocations

If you wish to master the calling of the quarters, it is very important to gain as much knowledge about their correspondences as possible. It is essential that your charge to summon each direction is more than just words on a page, learned by rote and repeated. There is no substitute for direct experience, and working some basic elemental magic will make the powers and entities of the four directions all the more real for you. Such knowledge will certainly enhance your work.

TO THE EAST, REALM OF DAWN

Begin with a simple meditation like the grounding and centering exercise given earlier. When contemplating the east, try to do this work at sunrise. Find an eastern-facing spot and rise early enough that you can see and feel the tranquil transition of the awakening world. This will give you a very real experience with the meaning of new beginnings as night surrenders her darkness to the power of the rising sun. Birds emerge from sleep and herald the start of the day. The grasses are wet with dew and the

A Witch's Grimoire

world seems fresh and undisturbed. Use this magical time to gain a fuller understanding of the east that you invoke. Write down your experience of your dawn meditation.

[?] What did you observe? How did you feel? These impressions based on your own experience will form the basis of your own original invocations.

_____

_____

_____

_____

_____

TO THE SOUTH, REALM OF HIGH NOON

Preferably on a bright and sunny day, begin your work experiencing the south. Find a space where you can sit quietly and relatively undisturbed as you breathe and envision the glowing center of energy contained within you as an internal echo of the sun itself. Face the south. Do not look directly into the sun overhead, but feel its heat and warmth on your face and shoulders. Notice the heightened activity of the day, when everything seems to be at its very peak. The sun gives life and life thrives in its presence. It is also dangerous. The power of the sun creates deserts and can burn our skin. Contemplate this duality of nurture and danger.

Book of Foundation

{ ? } Take note of your observations. When you understand these energies on an intimate level, your invocation of the south will come from a place of truth and experience.

_____

_____

_____

_____

TO THE WEST, REALM OF SUNSET

At the time of the setting sun, when the earth begins to grow quiet again, face the west. In many mythologies, the western lands are seen as a magical place. To the west lay the Summerlands, the Isle of Apples, Avalon, Tir na Nog, and the Isle of Man. Notice the changes in the sky. The sun drops lower toward the horizon, the temperature cools, and nocturnal creatures emerge from their sleep. Twilight covers the sky with many colors, and at last land and sea appear to be one.

{ ? } Write down your feelings as you relax and breathe deeply into the west, where day surrenders to night. Know that when you invoke the west, you are traveling to this place of twilight and mystery.

_____

_____

A Witch's Grimoire

TO THE NORTH, REALM OF MIDNIGHT

In the darkest hour of midnight, when the moon is bright and all are asleep, begin your meditation on the north. Gaze at the stars if you are so inclined. Find Polaris, the North Star, which has aided sailors and navigators for centuries. Know that once you find the North Star, you can never truly be lost. Picture the earth in the sleep of winter, trees bare of their leaves, the earth frozen and solid, icicles dangling from branch and twig. Know that you are standing upon the earth, the Great Mother who gave life to us all and who will one day ultimately cradle our bones. As the north pulls the compass point to itself, its magnetism and power are undeniable. When you call this direction, you are calling wisdom and knowledge. When you write your invocation of the north, the words will resonate on the spiritual plane, for you have experienced its essence firsthand.

[?] Write down your experience in this quiet hour of midnight and experience the solitude and tranquility of the north.

Book of Foundation

Awakening the Elemental Powers

Just as you have dedicated time and energy to gain pure knowledge of the directions, you should apply these same techniques to fully experiencing the elemental powers as well. The elemental powers embody the essence of all natural forces on the planet. Gaining knowledge and experience of them will strengthen your personal connection to nature. Likewise, the elemental powers are present physically and metaphorically within our own bodies, representing our bond with nature and our connection to the Goddess.

TO AIR, THE BREATH OF LIFE

To gain intimate experience with the spirits of air, you must trust your innate abilities and develop them so you are able to affect outcomes. You can do this through a spell called "Raising the Wind."

1. Begin by acknowledging the power within you. Find an open and natural area in which to work. Ideally, it should be relatively secluded so that you may have privacy and freedom from distractions such as the sounds of traffic and passersby.

2. Ground and center your energy. This process should by now be effective and second nature to you.

3. Hold your left hand in front of you with your palm facing right. You should be looking at your arm and thumb. Hold your right hand, fingers and palm straight and facing up, perpendicular to your left hand.

4. Move your right hand up and down, very close to but not touching your left hand. As the fingers of your right hand pass across your left palm, you may feel a cool sensation or a slight breeze. This is your life force, the same energy that is contained in the air that surrounds you. Familiarize

A Witch's Grimoire

yourself with this feeling and understand that this is the physical manifestation of your connection to the elements.

5. Switch hands and repeat this exercise until the feeling of power and energy radiating from your hands is undeniable. Now you are ready to begin.

6. Stand still and experience the air. Is it turbulent? Is it calm? What type of day is it? Is it clear and sunny, cloudy or blustery? Take a moment to reflect in silence.

7. Remember the power in your hands.

8. Face the east and hold your arms high over your head, your palms turned outward. Invite the wind to rise and blow over you. In one smooth and deliberate action, bring your arms down as you bend your knees, touching both of your hands to the earth and scooping up a little earth in each hand. Continue in a smooth motion, straightening your knees until you are standing upright, keeping your arms straight and swinging them in a wide arc in front of you, bringing them high over your head and flinging both handfuls of earth over each of your shoulders with as much strength as you have.

9. Repeat this three times, concentrating heavily on summoning the wind.

10. You can try this facing different directions, depending on the outcome you wish to influence. To conjure the winds of change and transformation, look to the east. To summon love and passion, turn to the south. To invoke the powers of healing and cleansing, call upon the west winds. For strength and prosperity, face the north.

Book of Foundation

After you have practiced this several times and over the course of several days, you will find that your results may improve.

[?] Were you able to raise the wind? Why do you think you were successful? Or what do you think prevented you from getting your desired outcome?

_____

_____

_____

_____

_____

TO FIRE, THE *SPIRIT OF PASSION*

Air is connected to fire in that the oxygen in the air is the food of fire that sustains it and enables it to grow. To understand fire, you must become accustomed to both its productive and its destructive qualities. Fire produces light that enables us to see in the darkness and heat that keeps us warm and cooks the food that nourishes our bodies. We use a candle flame as a symbol of hope when adversity strikes: To hold a candlelight vigil is to invoke divine intervention that seems to be the only possible way of holding on to hope. We light birthday candles to celebrate each passing year of life. To "carry a torch" for someone is to love him or her passionately. But we have also seen the destructive power of forest fires, which spread so rapidly and create so much devastation with incredible speed. Yet from the remaining ash the earth is fertilized, enabling new life to come forth and be nourished. Fire produces both physical and chemical changes. That which has been

A Witch's Grimoire

burned will never resemble its unburned state. Its composition will change, and it may be reduced to its purest form, carbon, which is the basic elemental component of our bodies and of the stars. Out of complete destruction arises absolute purification. Fire is a complicated element and deserves our meditation and reflection on its many attributes. Use the following exercise, "Embracing the Flame." Before attempting this exercise, thoroughly wash your hands to be sure they are free from any alcohol-based perfumes or other cosmetics that may be flammable.

1. Sit in darkness and light a single candle.

2. Begin this exercise by grounding and centering your energy, and by experiencing the life force that emanates from your hands, as described in "Raising the Wind."

3. Hold your hands over the candle flame, close enough that you can feel the heat, but not so close as to be burned or experience discomfort.

4. Notice how the candle illuminates the blood in your hands. Your hands may seem to glow red, showing the energy that they are surrounding.

5. With a smooth action, swiftly run your fingers directly through the flame. Your hand has just passed through fire, but if you do this quickly enough, you should feel no pain whatsoever. Repeat this gesture with your other hand until you have "embraced" the fire, felt its touch, and remained unharmed. This must be done quickly, taking only a second to avoid any potential for injury. Fire is a powerful element and is not to be trifled with.

6. Again cup your hands around the flame. Command the energy in your hands to affect the shape of the flame. Concentrate and see if you can

Book of Foundation

make it dance, or elongate, or move according to your will. Take your time and realize that success may only be achieved through repetition.

7. When your meditation is complete, do not blow out the candle. Wet your thumb and forefinger with your saliva and pinch out the flame. You may feel a slight sting from the heat of the flame or experience no discomfort at all. The important thing is to extinguish the flame by your own hand, sealing the energy within the candle so it will be contained therein for further magical workings instead of blowing the flame out and dissipating the energy.

[?] Were you able to make an impact on the size or direction of the flame? Could you feel the energy in your hands traveling through the fire? Was the heat comforting to you or did it make you uncomfortable?

_____

_____

_____

_____

_____

TO WATER, THE CRADLE OF LIFE

Just as our bodies are carbon based, aligning us with the purifying effects of fire, so too are we inextricably connected to the element of water. Water makes up a full 98 percent of our bodies. It is in the blood that runs through our veins, the sweat that cools us, the tears that fall in moments of joy and

A Witch's Grimoire

sorrow. Water is the cradle of life, the origin of all life on our planet. Yet at this point in our scientific evolution, we have more information about outer space than we do of the ocean depths. Water is the element of mystery, of emotion. Pulled by the gravitational force of the moon, the tides ebb and flow, and so does the blood of the womb, locked in a rhythmic dance attuned to the sea. We are creatures of water. We could live for only a few days without it. It is one of our most precious resources and its magical power is a force to be reckoned with.

Rain gives life to the crops of the field, but too much rain can destroy them. Rain can cleanse and nourish, but it can also drown. The ocean can be inviting, but also deadly. Like fire, water also possesses the duality of creation and destruction. Reflect on the awe-inspiring power of water and vow to use it only with the understanding of its duality and with respect for its great power. Familiarize yourself with its magical properties by using the following spell, "Waters of the Moon."

1. On the full moon if the night is clear and relatively cloudless, venture out of doors with a cup or chalice and a bottle of spring water.

2. Sit in a quiet spot. Ground and center your energy. Contemplate the pull of the moon on the tides.

3. Watch as the moon rises high in the sky. When the moon is at its zenith or as close as it will come to being overhead, open the bottle and pour the water into the cup. Set the cup on the ground in front of you. Try to position the cup so that the face of the moon is reflected on the surface of the water. This may take some maneuvering, even a change of location. If you do need to change your position, remember to ground and center your energy before you continue catching the moonbeam in the cup of water. When you are satisfied that the reflected light in the cup is coming from the moon, set the cup down and hold your hands around it.

4. Reflect on your own corporeal connection to the tides. The blood that flows through your veins is bound by the same natural laws as the oceans.

5. Direct the energy emanating from your hands into the water. Bring the cup to your lips and drink the water consecrated by the moonlight and your own power. Feel the power of the tides flowing through you as you drink. Take in the essence of water and understand the power it contains. Remember this power every time you call upon this element for assistance in your work.

[?] Were you able to see the moon in the water? How did it feel to drink in the energy of the moon?

_____

_____

_____

_____

_____

TO EARTH, THE BODY OF THE GODDESS

How does one begin to understand the awesome power of elemental earth? First realize that earth is the solid culmination of all the elements. At its center is the realm of fire. Great masses of molten magma churning around an iron core are forced upward through volcanoes and rise to create new lands. Seventy-five percent of the planet is covered by water,

A Witch's Grimoire

dominating the face of the globe. Surrounding the earth is the atmosphere of air and ozone, a protective shield against the ultraviolet rays of the sun.

Many witches use salt to symbolize the earth. Others carry actual bits of earth in a small pouch. You can also use gemstones or crystals, or even a simple river stone to attune with the earth.

1. Place your symbolic earth (salt, earth, or stone) upon your altar. Ground and center your energy, feeling the power in your hands.

2. Place your hands around your symbolic earth and transmit your desire for attunement into the object.

3. Pick up your symbolic earth carefully and hold it over your third eye, gently touching your forehead. Continue to breathe and feel the power of your pulse begin to grow.

4. You are now connected to the earth through the glowing core of fire that is your center, through the water you are mainly composed of that is one with the oceans, and through the air you breathe, the air that surrounds and touches all. Keep these connections in the forefront of your mind.

5. You will feel your pulse strengthen and vibrate in the symbol of earth you are holding. You are taking the charge of energy inherent in nature into yourself and, in turn, charging the earth with your own unique energy, melding into it with the understanding that you are interconnected now and always. The earth will be the source of your strength when you are in need. The earth will bless you with great bounty as you walk gently upon her. And after your death, she may cradle your bones.

[?] Were you able to attune with the earth? Which object did you choose to represent the earth? Could you feel your pulse within the symbolic earth?

Book of Foundation

Why or why not?

_____

_____

_____

_____

_____

Open the Circle

Just as you have used your inspiration and art to invoke the spirits of the directions and their corresponding elemental powers, you will also need to master the art of releasing them with the same strength of focus and elocution as when you called them in. After your work is done, give thanks and formally release the directions. Any time a magical working is enacted, there exists the possibility that residual energies will linger. Releasing the directions signifies that the working is considered complete. Thanks are given for any aid or assistance received, and the elemental powers are encouraged to return to their lovely realms. Choose your words with care, as they signify great power. Understand that any power or entity that is invoked but not released may very well remain.

A Witch's Grimoire

1. Face the north and raise your wand or athame. You can use the following releasing invocation as a starting point for creating your own:

Guardian of the Watchtowers of the North, Spirits of Earth!
We give thanks to you for your presence at this rite.
We ask now that the tremors of earthquakes recede back to the far corner of the universe from whence they came, ere you depart for your lovely realms.
Stay if you will, go if you must. Until we have need to call upon you again, to the North and the Spirits of Earth, we bid thee hail and farewell.

2. Walk to the west and raise your wand or athame, saying:

Guardian of the Watchtowers of the West, Spirits of Water!
We give thanks to you for your presence at this rite.
We ask now that the mighty waves subside and that the tides ebb and recede back to the far corner of the universe from whence they came, ere you depart for your lovely realms.
Stay if you will, go if you must. Until we have need to call upon you again, to the West and the Spirits of Water, we bid thee hail and farewell.

3. Turn to the south, again raising your wand or athame, saying:

Guardian of the Watchtowers of the South, Spirits of Fire!
We give thanks to you for your presence at this rite.
We ask now that the raging flames die down to gently glowing embers as you recede back to the far corner of the universe from whence you came, ere you depart for your lovely realms.

Book of Foundation

Stay if you will, go if you must. Until we have need to call upon you again, to the South and the Spirits of Fire, we bid thee hail and farewell.

4. Finally, walk to the east and raise your wand or athame, saying:

Guardian of the Watchtowers of the East, Spirits of Air!
We give thanks to you for your presence at this rite.
We ask now that the winds of change subside into gentle breezes as they recede back to the far corner of the universe from whence they came, ere you depart for your lovely realms.
Stay if you will, go if you must. Until we have need to call upon you again, to the East and the Spirits of Air, we bid thee hail and farewell.

Practice these dismissals until they become second nature. As you progress through the exercises given earlier, it will be easier for you to call in and release the directions with invocations of your own.

Write your invocations and releasings in your grimoire. In the true tradition of the grimoire, yours should have the basic traditional invocations that you have reworked into your own voice.

Combine the Elemental Powers in a Sacred Spiral

Now that you have a good understanding of the importance of the elemental powers and how they are used in magic, here is an easy bread recipe you can apply to combine the four elements to create actual, physical nourishment. Even if you aren't a kitchen witch, it is very important for any priestess worth her salt to be able to do this for practical knowledge and for ceremonial use. It may take all day, but the results will be worth it.

Ingredients and Materials Needed
- Medium-size mixing bowl
- Large mixing bowl
- Fork
- Spoon
- Cutting board or other flat surface
- Clean kitchen towel
- Two 8-inch round pans, greased
- Knife
- ¼ cup of warm water
- Few pinches sugar
- Two ¼-ounce packages active dry yeast
- 1 tablespoon salt
- ¼ cup honey
- 4 tablespoons (or half a stick) of butter
- 1 cup water
- 1 cup milk
- 3+ cups unbleached flour

1. Put the quarter cup of warm water in the medium-size mixing bowl. Add a few pinches of sugar. Let the sugar dissolve in the warm water.

2. Add to the sugar-water mix two packages of active dry yeast and set aside. This will become the basis of the air element that will cause your loaf to rise.

3. In large bowl, combine 1 tablespoon of salt, ¼ cup of honey, and 4 tablespoons (or half a stick) of butter. With a fork, mix these ingredients until they are thoroughly blended and indistinguishable from each other.

4. Over low heat on the stovetop, combine 1 cup of water and 1 cup of milk; together, they represent the water element. Heat so the mixture is hot but be careful not to boil or overheat or you will burn the milk.

5. Pour the hot water and milk into the large bowl. Stir the mixture gently for a few minutes so that the butter, salt, and honey blend dissolves.

6. Add the yeast along with the ¼ cup of sweetned water that is activating the yeast. Let this mixture stand undisturbed for five minutes. The yeast should be multiplying and visibly growing.

7. Add 3 cups of unbleached flour, the earth element, mixing it in with a spoon. Continue adding flour, no more than 1 cup at a time, until the mixture begins to resemble a ball and starts to pull away from the sides of the bowl.

8. When the mixture begins to get too heavy to turn with a spoon, you will need to mix with your hands. Sprinkle some flour

onto a cutting board or other surface, and cover your hands with flour as well. Put the ball of dough onto the board or surface and begin kneading it. Keep adding flour as you turn the ball of dough over and over to keep it from sticking to your hands or other surfaces. Press the heel of your palm into the dough and then pull the dough back over itself. Fold the dough in half, rotate it clockwise forty-five degrees, and press into it again.

9. Begin to develop a rhythm to the kneading. Each time you turn the dough, envision it passing through each direction, consecrated by little circles of its own. As you press your hands into the dough, let good intentions and energy travel through your hands. Continue kneading for about ten minutes, adding flour as necessary, and let the dough rest a while.

10. Wash out the bowl you used to make the base of the bread and dry it thoroughly.

11. Coat the surface of the bowl with butter. Put the ball of dough into the buttered bowl, turn it over once, and let it rest. This will keep the dough from sticking to the bowl.

12. Cover the bowl with a clean kitchen towel and put it in a warm place such as a sunny window.

13. Let the dough rise in this warm place until the ball has doubled in size. This normally takes about two hours.

14. Once the dough has doubled in size, take your fist and punch the center of the risen dough to deflate it. Fold the dough over itself so that it forms a ball once again.

15. Grease the two 8-inch round pans with butter and set aside.

16. Turn the dough back onto the floured surface and cut in two. Knead the dough gently so that two distinct loaves are forming.

17. Take the first loaf and stretch it out, rolling it into an oblong shape as you stretch.

18. Once the dough is stretched out, begin twisting it little by little. Begin at one end and keep twisting until you reach the other end. When the elongated dough has been twisted and is lying flat in a straight line, take one end and pull it clockwise to start creating a spiral. Pinch it so that it curls inward and sticks to itself. Continue turning the twisted loaf around this point until you have made a round spiral. Pinch the outer edge to the inside to keep from unrolling.

19. Place the spiral loaf in one of the round pans.

20. Repeat this same technique with the other ball of dough until you have two beautiful spirals.

21. Cover both loaves with a towel and let them rise again until they are double in size; this takes usually about an hour or maybe a little less.

22. Heat the oven to 400° and place both loaves on the oven rack, releasing them to the fire element. Bake for about thirty minutes, or until golden brown. (Baking kills the action of the yeast and stops it from growing.)

23. Test the loaves by tapping on them. They will sound hollow when done. Allow the loaves to cool thoroughly before removing them from the pans.

A Witch's Grimoire

Witness the wonder of transformation that you have caused to occur. You have taken the four elements, consecrated them, and combined them to create food for your body. Your magic is able to sustain life. You can use this loaf as an offering to the Goddess or for ritual feasting, or both. Once you have mastered this basic recipe, feel free to experiment with it by adding ingredients. Preparing for a Samhain feast? Add a cup of cooked pumpkin to the dough as you knead it. Want to make Ostara particularly festive this year? After the bread cools, tuck little nasturtium blossoms in the folds of the spiral for a beautiful and edible garnish. The only limit to the possibilities and combinations is your own creativity.

3

Book of Changes

What does it mean to practice magic? In Wicca, we see magic as the natural forces that bind our lives. Take some time to think about why practicing magic is important to you. Write your thoughts in your grimoire. Begin to define what you believe. Once you put something in writing, you can be objective about its truth. While magic is by nature as limitless as the imagination, it should always be grounded and based in reality. Do you seek out magic as a way to escape from the mundane aspects of life? What do you find to be the dominant aspects of your magical practice? Are you more concerned with affecting your personal life (love, career, money)? Or are you seeking to deepen your spiritual connection to the universe? Is your magic based in obtaining practical results or enhancing intuition?

Most likely, your magic is a combination of all of these. Writing down your ideas and desires helps to clarify them. A Wiccan or witch does not seek to send sparks flying from her fingertips, nor does she seek to levitate objects and hurl them through space. Instead, she uses her attunement and eventual influence over the forces of nature to elicit a series of controlled coincidences that will achieve a desired result. A witch seeks to move, bend, or otherwise change the natural flow of energy in the universe to bring about a condition that will benefit herself and in turn all other beings as well. Ethical witches abide by the "law of three." Whatever intention and energy is sent out is returned to the sender threefold. This is a strong deterrent against mischief, manipulation, or other kinds of deceptive practice. You will only be able to truly observe the results of your work if you write down your spells from beginning to outcome. Effective spells must have a structure, and you cannot evaluate your structure without first recording it.

Magic: Theory and Practice

The theory and practice of magic can be described as consistent ritual technique. Some of the most familiar forms of magic found in Wicca originated in southern Europe. The ancient peoples of the Mediterranean region practiced what has evolved today into what we think of as spell casting. The typical structure of an effective spell involves five basic steps, each step with its own specific function.

The first step is *preparation.* The preparation involves clearly stating your intention as to why this magical work is absolutely necessary. Selecting an auspicious time is also part of the preparation. This includes working under the appropriate phase of the moon and considering any significant astrological influences, as well as time of year and time of day. Finally, preparation includes gathering the appropriate tools specific to the work at hand. Herbs are gathered or purchased and tools are consecrated with the intention of ceremonial use.

The next step is *casting the circle,* as described in the previous chapter. The circle is cast as a container for the magical energy as well as a shield to protect the witch from distraction. Anything done within the confines of sacred space is considered set apart from uninvited influences.

Book of Changes

After the circle is cast, the *appropriate deity is invoked.* Depending on your needs and your desired result, a specific aspect of a goddess or god will be invoked and invited into the sacred space. If you're working outdoors, the deity may manifest through a sign or natural occurrence, such as a clap of thunder if the day is stormy or even the parting of clouds, an increase in the wind, or other such phenomena. Sometimes the token spirit animal associated with the deity also appears. The deity may manifest in other, subtler, ways as well. Sometimes the goddess will speak directly in the form of an oracle.

Whatever the mode of manifestation, once the divine presence is established, the *petition or plea is made.* In medieval times, it was not unusual for the witch to command the spirit, or to even threaten the deity into carrying out the will of the witch, but this practice has been widely abandoned in modern times.

The final step is *thanking and releasing the deity and opening the circle*, trusting that the goddess is infinitely wise and the spell will reach its destination.

The second ritual structure originated in the northern regions of Europe, from the Germanic tribes, and is referred to as "the charm" as opposed to "the spell." The charm differs from the spell in many ways. While no less structured, the charm is certainly less formal. Tools are gathered and consecrated, but there is generally not the same level of preparation involved in conjuring a charm as opposed to casting a spell. Although a goddess or god may be invoked, they are viewed as *aiding* the will of the practitioner, rather than *achieving* the work for them. In spell work, there is an emphasis on invoking divine assistance, whereas in charm work, the emphasis is placed on the person who is doing the work. Think of the different manifestations of power to aid you in understanding this distinction. Power may be bestowed by the Goddess, and empowerment can also come from within. It is this inner power that one seeks to tap into to aid the work of the charm. Additionally, since there is no need for protection when casting a charm, there is no need for banishing. The three basic elements of the charm are the following:

A Witch's Grimoire

- Symbols, insignia, and signs
- Spoken or written words
- Herbs, oils, or other necessary substances

The symbols act as conduits, or doorways, through which a goddess may enter. While the symbols may not have any intrinsic power, the power we give them comes from the combination of meaning and intention. Only when our intention is focused and specific can any kind of precise result be attained. When we speak our intention, we project energy into the symbol. Without the power of the word, the symbol is devoid of any real power. In this sense, the verbal elements are inextricably bound to the very things they name. *As it is written (or spoken), so must it be done.*

In charm work, there is a heavier emphasis placed on the person working the magic. The mindset of the witch at work is the most important element in determining the success or failure of the charm. The way in which the herbs and oils are handled, the conviction with which the incantation is spoken, and the energy imparted into the symbols will have a greater impact on the outcome than anything else including time of day or phase of the moon.

The Magical Tools

If you have raised your wand to call in the directions, if you have ever cut another covener in or out of the circle, if you have poured a libation, you are no doubt comfortable with many of the working tools of Wicca. But have you taken the time to draw a connection between yourself and your tool? If you have, do you remember what you did and said?

Taking the time to invent and record original consecrations of your tools will strengthen your connections to them. When you write a consecration in your grimoire, you have made a personal investment of energy in both your

Book of Changes

book and in your tool. This investment of energy will enhance your work by allowing you to draw on inspiration every time you use a magical tool.

The Wand

As we call upon the east, the realm of new beginnings, and invoke the air, it is appropriate to take up the wand. The wand is the corresponding tool to the air element and its use is for invoking the gentler, more ethereal spirits such as the faeries or Sidhe.

Because of its basic phallic shape, the wand is often thought to represent the male principle, but it does not truly have a specific gender attachment.

Usually, the wand is one of the witch's own making. It should be the length from the inside of one's elbow to the tip of the index finger. It is traditionally recommended that the material for the wand be cut from a living branch in a single stroke, and then a symbolic offering made to the tree who generously bestows the shaft that will become the wand.

Often, the wand is carved with symbols, astrological or otherwise, or adorned with gems. Many wands are tipped with a quartz crystal, a highly sensitive stone used for sending and receiving energy as well as messages.

Some wands are made of copper, another highly conductive substance, and wands may even be hollow, with gems and symbols concealed within.

When you craft your wand, or if you possess it already, it is still necessary to consecrate it as a sacred tool. The wand represents the power of the will, and through understanding the uses of the wand you will find that you are able to invoke the spirits more effectively.

Think about the work you have already done in respect to getting in touch with the element of air and the east and use this experience to write a consecration for your wand.

[?] If you have owned and used your consecrated wand for many years, describe in your grimoire how it came to you, the process you used to craft it, what type of material it was made from, or who gave it to you. Revisit the day you found your wand and record as many details as you can remember. If you used a specific consecration, include it as well.

___

___

___

___

___

The Athame

The corresponding tool to elemental fire and the spirits of the south is the athame. Representing the male principle, the athame is a black-handled knife with a dull or blunted double-edged blade. The blade will rarely, if ever, need to be sharpened because the athame is exclusively a ceremonial ritual tool and rarely actually cuts any kind of physical object. Its purpose is to cast the circle and cut a door to allow people in and out of the circle. Occasionally, witches will use the athame for scribing seals on candles, or other ritual-inspired tasks, but many refuse to use the athame for any purpose other than symbolic ritual gestures. There is an old superstition that originates in the Saxon tradition that the athame should never be given from one person to another, as this would sever the friendship.

It is customary for the witch to craft or procure her own athame and reserve it solely for personal use. The athame consists of a basic structure: the double-edged blade; the hilt, which is in between the blade and the handle; the tang, which protrudes into the handle and keeps the blade

Book of Changes

secure; and the handle itself, which may or may not be finished off with a pommel on the end. The handle of the athame is traditionally black and carved with symbols, usually only the pentagram and witch's craft name or another appropriate insignia that resonates with the owner. The athame is dedicated at the time of the witch's initiation and is never used by any other person.

[?] Think about the responsibility that comes with wielding a blade, even if the knife is chiefly symbolic. Take time to explore in your mind the elemental connections to this tool. Write an original consecration for your athame.

_____

_____

_____

_____

_____

The Chalice

Perhaps the most romanticized of all the ritual tools, the chalice appropriately represents the water element and the female principle. The chalice is the vessel of energy that contains the magic. While it can be said that the purpose of the wand is to direct energy inward and toward the circle, and the athame to protect from without the circle, the chalice serves as a containment device for keeping sacred vibrations within. It is used in ritual as a cup, often filled with water, wine, or fruit juice. Libations to the earth and to a goddess or god are poured from it, and it is often passed around the circle for practitioners to raise a cup to honor the divine presence in their lives. The cup is raised in thanks, offered with solemnity, and shared with joy.

Most often, the chalice is a stemmed cup of silver, representing the connection to the moon. The chalice can also be glass or earthenware; any natural substance in tune with the vibrations of the elements is acceptable. Just as water represents the emotions, think of the chalice as the cradle of the emotions. Your wishes and dreams are contained within it. The sacred energy with which the contents of the cup are charged are enclosed and ultimately poured forth.

[?] Get in touch with your emotions and the power they contain. Meditate on the aspects of water, the feel of the cup in your hands, and its intended sacred use. Write an original consecration for your chalice.

_____

_____

_____

_____

_____

The Pentacle

Representing the element of earth, the pentacle is one of the most revered and misunderstood symbols from the Wiccan tradition. The pentacle is a five-pointed star contained within a circle and often embellished around the outer edges with astrological symbols or other insignia. The five-pointed star, or pentagram, represents the human form in perfection: mind and body

Book of Changes

in graceful harmony, the intellect in balance with the extremities. Perhaps the most famous of all pentacles is Leonardo DaVinci's rendering of the "Microcosmic Man," in which a male figure is imposed over the pentagram and then contained within the defining boundaries of the circle.

In addition to the individuality represented by the pentagram, the circle of the pentacle represents wholeness and oneness with the universe. The pentacle is also said to be a symbol of the encapsulation of all elements and although it does not represent a specific gender, its energy is often considered to be female.

In ritual, the pentacle is made of metal, wood, or earthenware and is placed on the altar in the north. The salt is consecrated on it and offerings are placed on it.

In modern times, we sometimes see the inverted pentagram used as a symbol of evil; however, nothing could be further from the truth. While it is true that placing the pentacle at different orientations carries different meanings, none of these associations are baneful. Most often, the upright pentacle indicates protective energies; it's a type of psychic shield. In the inverted position, the pentacle indicates receptive energies, or things that we wish to call to us. These meanings carry no value judgments. Any value will come from the intention of the person using the pentacle.

Think of the sheer scope of what this symbol represents. Remember that your pentacle is also a practical tool. It will be frequently used in ritual, and may get wax drippings on it, wine spilled on it, and salt poured on it. It will often require cleaning.

[?] Think of your connection to the earth and write an original consecration for your pentacle here.

_____

_____

OTHER TOOLS OF THE CRAFT

As you move along your spiritual path, you will come across and perhaps choose to adopt other kinds of tools, including the following:

- Besom, or broom
- Bolline, or white-handled knife
- Cauldron
- Sword
- Censer
- Bell
- Scourge
- Cord
- Witch's Ladder
- Mirror

Any tool that enhances your magical practice deserves the same amount of reverence as the essential elemental working tools. With each tool you incorporate, be sure to write a few lines about it in your grimoire.

Consecrate Your Working Tools

As you continue to build your collection of magical tools, think of them in much the same way as you do your grimoire. They are ritual tools reserved for specific and sacred purposes. Once you have consecrated a tool for

Book of Changes

magical work, you have essentially changed it. You have changed your perception of the tool, you have changed your relationship to the tool, and you have changed the manner in which you handle, use, and store your tool.

Which of these tools do you already possess? How did you acquire them? In what manner did you spiritually dedicate their purpose? Are there tools listed here that you feel would aid you that you do not yet possess? How do you plan to acquire them? Using the elemental correlations described earlier, write down original consecrations for all of the tools you already have. As you write the consecrations, think about the following things:

Intended use of the tool

_____

_____

Elemental correspondences

_____

_____

Directional correspondences

_____

_____

Deities that you associate with these energies

_____

_____

A Witch's Grimoire

Goddesses and gods you will invoke to charge the tools

_____

_____

Ingredients you will need to procure

_____

_____

Appropriate lunar phase for the work at hand

_____

_____

Put Theory into Practice

Now that you are versed in the structure of spellcraft, it is time to turn what you have learned into practical experience that is derived from working knowledge and not mere book learning.

THE WASHING SPELL

A powerful and important basic spell is that of self-blessing and cleansing. This is best done alone on a full moon night.

1. Begin by drawing a ritual bath. Make sure the temperature of the water is pleasant. You may decoct an infusion of rose petals and lavender to add to the water.

2. You may wish to begin the cleansing ritual by burning incense or

Book of Changes

white sage as the tub fills. Let the smoke waft over your body, enjoying its aroma while taking care not to deeply inhale the smoke.

3. Release your mundane cares and get in touch with your center of power. As you bathe, visualize yourself in a state of wholeness and completeness, in perfect health, with acute mental faculties, at peace, and in love with the universe.

4. You may recite the following verses, adapted from a medieval Icelandic grimoire called the *Galdrabòk*, translated by Stephen Flowers. This verse and the protection verse are not as they appear in the original translation. In the tradition of the grimoire, they have been inspired by the authentic, and then altered to apply to the Wiccan philosophy, but their origin is from the medieval Germanic practitioners of ceremonial magic.

> I wash myself in thy dew and dales
> In the brilliance of thy fire, my Lady
> I set thy blessed form between my eyes
> I wash away all of my foes and their spells
> I wash away from myself the power and the anger of men
> The world shall be kind to me, with friends and kind deeds
> The earth shall be gracious to me in goods and in acquisitions
> Everything will be successful that I need to do, to speak, to think
> This I do bid thee, Lady, Queen of Heaven, so that everyone who sees me today will have to cast kind glances at me and will be delighted with me
> Likewise, I bid thee, Mother of the Gods, Divine Creatrix,
> That thou will turn away from me and remove all ruin and ill luck
> All malice and treachery on the part of others who want

to deceive me in words and through words, in deeds and through deeds, or in whatever way that they seek to ruin me.
Hear thou my need, blessed Goddess. I have faith in thee and I trust in all good things. So mote it be.

5. After you get out of your bath and dry yourself off, stand naked before your altar and give yourself a personal blessing, adapted from the "traditional" five-fold self-blessing:

In the name of the Goddess of Ten Thousand Names,
Bless my eyes, that I may have clarity of vision
Bless my mouth, that I may speak only truth
Bless my heart, that I may love and be loved
Bless my sex, that I may know pleasure
Bless my feet, that I may continue to walk in your ways.

THE PROTECTION SPELL

Before you begin the protection spell, cast a circle, call in the directions using your own original invocations, and invite a goddess or god to witness your work as you ask for their protection.

1. This protection verse also has its origins in the *Galdrabòk*, but I have adapted it to suit the modern Wiccan sensibility:

Hear thou me, Triple Goddess, Sacred Maiden, Blessed Mother, Crone of Wisdom, Creatrix of all things, and thy blessed Consort, the Sun King, who rides his fiery chariot across the sky. Be thou a shield for my soul, my life, and my body; inside as well as outside, for seeing and hearing, tasting, smelling, and feeling, for flesh and for blood, veins, and sinews, cartilage and bone, bowels, and

Book of Changes

all my body's movements and connections. Indeed for thy name's sake may all my joints and limbs receive life and spirit, to move, and be strengthened, and become whole. Protect me, Lord and Lady, on the right and left sides, forward and backward, above and below, from the inside and outside, when I bow down, and when I rise up. In hard weather, in waters great and small, in the sea in high waves and in confusing darkness; when I am walking, standing, sitting, in sleep and while awake, in silence and while talking, and in all my body's workings. Protect me from deadly dangers that threaten from land, from the waters and sea, from all beasts and creatures of the ocean, birds and beasts that go on four feet and all creeping beasts. Protect me, Lord and Lady, from all evil, from fire and claps of thunder, from snow and hail, from rain and wind, from earthquakes and all kinds of movement in the earth; from poison, from all glances from envious eyes, from evil words and works, and dangerous situations. Protect me from all the hostility of the enemy who wants to withhold all good things, here before death, and in death, and in the other world after death. Thou Goddess and God who live in perfect balance through all the ages, so mote it be.

2. Meditate in perfect silence for a while. Reflect on the words of power you have spoken. Feel the transformative powers begin to take effect. Notice in both of these verses how utterly specific they are.

3. Observe the subtle changes in your perception, how different you feel now that you have treated yourself as a sacred being. Bask in the presence of the divine reality and thank the Goddess and the God for their presence at your ritual. You may substitute the names of goddesses and gods with whose energy you feel the need to work for the honorific titles used in the verses given above.

4. When you feel that you have allowed enough time for the spell to take effect, it is time to release the deities invoked and to release the directions as well. It is very important that the spirits be released with as much eloquence and reverence as when you called them in.

THE BANISHING SPELL

You are by now accustomed to methods of clearing a physical space in order to prepare for spiritual workings. Part of your awareness of undesirable influences and your ability to deal with them will arise out of what naturally happens when you grow accustomed to recognizing energies that are beyond the normal din of everyday life. There will be times when you will find it necessary to effectively banish an unwanted entity, be it the residual energy from an unfortunate event, an unpleasant memory that arises after a confrontation with someone from your past who may have harmed you, or a psychic disturbance of some kind. This banishing spell includes powerful invocations to the archangels. Many Wiccans use angels in their magical work, as the use of angels predates Judeo-Christian practice.

1. Begin with a ritual bath with the strong intention of cleansing away unwanted energy. Remember that the energy you put into forming your intention will have a significant influence on the outcome of your actions. If you prepare the bath with nothing more than physical cleansing in mind, then you will most likely achieve just that and nothing more. Draw the bath, add an infusion of your favorite herbs, and let it steep a while.

2. Go to your altar and use your athame to place three heaps of salt upon the pentacle.

3. Consecrate the salt and cast it into the bathwater, envisioning all of the energy you have imbued into the salt dissolving into the water and

surrounding you. Salt has intense purification associations and with a good consecration, you can maximize its effectiveness.

4. As you bathe in the purified waters, allow your mind to transcend all undesirable influences. Allow your spirit to rise up. Send your energy to the feet of the great Goddess, to a place far beyond the reach of any harm, real or imagined.

5. After this meditation, dry and dress yourself (if you wish to) and enter your temple space.

6. Burn white sage or frankincense to clear the room, and take up your athame or sword.

7. Point the blade directly in front of you and slowly turn clockwise around the circle. As you turn, clearly envision a line of fire emanating from the tip of the blade and surrounding the border of the circle. As you pass each direction, firmly speak the following charge:

As the archangel Gabriel stands before me
Undesired guest, unwanted presence, I banish thee!
May the gale force winds of the frozen North
Tear thee from me and cast ye forth
May the mighty earth with all her power
Assist me in this needful hour
So that once thou art from me swept away
Encased in stone forever thou will stay
And by the law of three times three
For the good of all I banish thee
This charm never to rebound on me
As I do will, so must it be!

A Witch's Grimoire

As the archangel Raphael stands behind me
Undesired one, unwanted guest, I banish thee
As sure as the moon doth wax and wane
Thou art swept away by the fire's flame
Unto me thou will never return
Nor unto another, for truly ye will burn
Until only a harmless ash remains
To be washed away by a cleansing rain
For the good of all this charge I lay
A day turns to night and night turns to day
I banish thee by three times three
As I do will, so must it be!
As the archangel Michael stands to my right
I banish thee with all my might
Unwanted one from me be gone
And be consumed in the fire of dawn
May the turbulent winds of the sirocco rise
And sweep your sight far from my eyes
The wind from the east may never cease
To keep thee away and never release thee
Bound that ye may do no harm
I banish thee by sacred charm.
The archangel Uriel guards me from the left side
Thou will find no shelter, no place to hide
The force of the oceans will pull thee away
On the floor of the ocean shall ye ever stay
The tides will draw thee into the deep
Never to wake and never to sleep
But dissolve into the great abyss
By the strength of the charm, I promise this
To cast you into the deepest sea

Book of Changes

For the good of all I banish thee
This charm never to rebound on me
As I do will, so must it be!

A WORD ABOUT RHYMES

Never underestimate the power of the spoken word, particularly if it is spoken in rhyme. Spells and charms spoken in rhyme have a special power, and this power lends itself to enhance the efficacy of the working.

The rhythm of a verse also helps to build the effectiveness of the spell by linking it to the sacred vibration. Rhythm is inherent in nature. It is the percussion of the heartbeat, the beat of the pulse as life courses through the veins. It is the sound of waves crashing against the shore, as they have done since the beginning of time. It connects us to the here and now, at the same time allowing us to explore what lies outside of ourselves and that which is eternal.

Craft Your Own Spells

You may have noticed during the purification and protection rituals that much of a ritual's effectiveness is due to its being specific. Always remember this when crafting and casting a spell. Separate these two endeavors and relate them as separate entities to remind you to think before you speak: Carefully plan your spells before you attempt to cast them. The old adage, "be careful what you ask for, you just might get it," is never more relevant than in spell work. You must consider the implications of every nuance—the color of the candles you choose to place on the altar, the manner in which you have prepared your tools, the conviction with which you consecrate and invoke, every word that you speak, and especially, the intention in your mind.

A Witch's Grimoire

As you continue to deepen your knowledge and explore the structure of spellcraft, you will be creating your own original spells and charms. Through this work, you will gain greater confidence and a more personal understanding of the connections between word and deed. You will be able to observe the results that manifest after you perform a magical working, and see if what you do really works.

Always be aware of the link between thought and action, gesture and intention, and how they relate to the karmic repercussions of the law of three. The energy you send out will return to you threefold. It is thus in your absolute best interest to remember that a spell that is not carefully planned and thoroughly examined before it is cast into the world may have unexpected or very undesirable results that you didn't intend. It is very important for you to use your grimoire as a workbook to build the framework of the spells you wish to create:

- Write down your ideas and give them time to settle.
- Make a list of ingredients for a charm and then research the charm's implications.
- Look for ways to make your invocations more specific.
- Approach your work from a place of patience and wisdom rather than the need for immediate gratification.
- Try to anticipate what the possible outcomes may be, then cast a spell or work a charm that will truly be of benefit to all beings.

Just as important, allow sufficient time for outcomes to reveal themselves and record what happens honestly and accurately. Sometimes you will be able to observe results immediately and dramatically; sometimes it may take a few days, or even a few changes of the moon. The amount of time it takes for an outcome to manifest is not necessarily a measure of the success of the magical work. Soon, you will begin to see patterns that help you decide which techniques result in effective spell casting and which do not.

Book of Changes

Make a copy of the following worksheet to keep track of your spells and charms. Write in pencil and revise them frequently. Record what happens every time you work the spell or charm. Any spells that work well for you should then be transferred, word for word, into your grimoire.

Preparation

Intention, stated as clearly and as specifically as possible

_____

_____

Phase of the moon best suited to this type of work

_____

_____

Other astrological and planetary influences

_____

_____

Time of day appropriate to work this spell

_____

_____

A Witch's Grimoire

Divination techniques used to determine the surrounding influences of the situation you desire to affect (Tarot, runes, etc.)

_____

_____

Divinatory results

_____

_____

Execution

Goddesses and gods invoked

_____

_____

Herbs and/or essential oils used

_____

_____

Manner in which they were used

_____

_____

Book of Changes

Colors worn, or colors of altar cloth, candles, etc.

_____

_____

Manifestation

Date and time spell was cast

_____

_____

Results attributed to this spell

_____

_____

Time elapsed between casting spell and manifestation of outcome.

_____

_____

A Witch's Grimoire

It is a good idea to make multiple copies of this page in order to keep track of your spell crafting in a thorough and consistent manner. After you have created a spell, you may find that its reach is too broad, or perhaps not broad enough. Be objective about your work before attempting the spell. You may find that your needs have changed since the original inception. It is also important that your work is coming from a place of positive and confident action, and not merely as a reaction to any given set of circumstances.

Above all, remember that you will only get out of a spell or charm as much as you put into it. Whether you are casting a spell for yourself or on behalf of another, the need for specifically stating the intention and contemplating the energy that will rebound will not change. It may be said that it is even more important to be specific when performing a magical working for someone else because you are somewhat removed from the direct effects of the outcome. Always craft your spells and charms with the knowledge that what you send out will indeed return to you. Do not send out an energy that you are not prepared to receive yourself, even if it is on behalf of someone else.

4

Book of Visions

When you prepare yourself to enact a ritual or cast a spell or a charm, you are agreeing to suspend reality for a period of time to get in touch with energies greater than your own limited scope of individual perception. By entering the space and time "between the worlds," you make an agreement with yourself and with the spirits. You agree to acknowledge their divine presence by inviting them into your sacred space. You agree to accept physical manifestations of the divine presence. And you agree to suspend your sense of disbelief in order to accept that magic and psychic experiences are indeed possible and even desirable. For some, this may prove to be difficult, as the rational mind often requires some type of proof that a spiritual experience has occurred. If you go into a magical working knowing that you will not be satisfied with anything less than an obvious, undeniable message from beyond, you may thus be disappointed. You will not get a clap of thunder in assurance that the goddesses and gods have acknowledged your work. But, then again, you just might.

Creative Visualization

Rather than focusing on immediate outcomes and instantaneous validation, it is much more desirable to develop your intuitive abilities so that you will be able to interpret the more subtle changes that the Goddess is known for working in our lives and to recognize the divine presence and accept it as reality.

While imagination is at the heart of ritual, we know that if the mind is unable to conceive of a situation or state of being, it will certainly never attain it. When we imagine the possibilities of what we may be able to create, the first seeds of a desired possibility becoming reality are planted. One way to achieve a deeper understanding of your own magical practice is by doing just that: *practicing*! Creative visualization is designed to improve your psychic abilities as you use your imagination. It is a necessary building block in the skills you will need to make your magic most effective. Once you can clear your psyche as well as your psychic space, you can focus on a detailed meditation to expand your imagination so that your mind is open and ready to create. Creative visualization should put you more in touch with your Craft.

It is best if you can sit comfortably in a trance-like state and have someone read this visualization to you. If this is not possible, read it silently to yourself, pausing after every few lines to develop clear images in your mind before proceeding. When you are finished, answer the questions that follow to see how vividly you were able to imagine this circumstance.

INTO THE GROVE

This exercise is designed to put you more in touch with lunar energies. It may be done indoors or outdoors, and it is best performed on a full moon night, though any night will do. The purposes of this exercise are to give you the opportunity to see yourself as a part of the divine matrix of life, to activate your imagination, and to enable you to concentrate on the precision of detail that effective spell casting requires.

- Sit in a comfortable position that you will be able to sustain for a while. Close your eyes and take a deep breath. Hold your breath for a second and then exhale slowly and completely. Continue breathing in a relaxed, easy manner. Form a mental picture of your immediate surroundings. Allow your imagination to enable them to disintegrate. Gone are the tables and chairs, curtains and walls. Gone are the telephone, the television, and all the trappings of the waking world. Let your mind create new surroundings, reflections of the natural world. The door to the room you are in is then replaced by the pathway to a new reality.

- You are standing at the edge of the woods. The sun has set long ago and the night is cool and clear. You see a path before you and you feel compelled to follow it.

- The sounds of the night are all around you like a natural orchestra. Crickets provide the string section, a chorus of cicadas dominates the treble notes, and an elusive owl contributes the occasional solo. You are comforted by this symphony, knowing that you are not alone but in the peaceful company of nature's creatures.

- The moon is rising high in the sky, casting shadows all around you. You are drawn in by instinct, not knowing where you are headed, but knowing that some intriguing mystery awaits you. You are on unfamiliar ground, but you are not afraid.

- The cool night air surrounds you and comforts you. You feel strangely at home, as though you were walking through a pleasant childhood memory—some special place that only you and maybe a trusted friend knew about.

A Witch's Grimoire

- You feel as though you are traveling through time with every step you take. Each step on the path takes you deeper into the woods and farther from home, and yet you have rarely felt so at peace. You feel as though you are being led through these woods, that some unknown destiny is calling you toward itself.

- You have lost track of time. It seems that you have been walking for hours, yet you feel no effects of exhaustion or weariness.

- The path widens and you come to a small clearing. There is a pond before you, surrounded by thirteen trees. You recognize many of them: oak, willow, ash, hawthorn, and birch. You realize that you are in a sacred grove and that the trees are here to protect and guard you.

- The pond beckons you to gaze into the still waters and you happily oblige. You walk to the water's edge and expect to see your own reflection. Instead, you see only the mirror of the night sky above with the radiant white moon reflected back at you. You are mesmerized by the sight of moonlight on the water.

- The pond is so still and the air around you is so vibrant and alive. It seems as if the moon's reflection is close enough to touch. You reach out and run your fingertips across the surface of the pool, sending ripples that spread outward. The moonlight responds by dancing for you, shimmering through the circles your fingertips have created, and then gradually becoming still again.

- You look upward toward the sky, amazed at the clearness of the night and the brightness of the moon. She seems so very far away and unattainable, like a delicious dream from which you do not wish to awaken.

Book of Visions

- The sounds around you remind you that you are very much awake and experiencing this peacefulness with full clarity and lucidity.

- The moon looms, shining and large, and seems closer to you than it did a moment ago. You feel the cool night breeze across your skin.

- You look around and even the trees seem closer. You can see the branches vividly as though you are moving upward, yet you feel as though you have not moved at all.

- The moon draws you closer. You are now eye level with the very tops of the trees.

- The sky opens before you; vast, perfect darkness, strewn with stars. It is as if you are looking the great Goddess directly in the eye. The expanse of black sky is nothing more than the pupil of her eye and the brilliant moon is but a glimmer of knowledge and recognition.

- You ascend higher and higher. The earth is now very far away and you are surrounded in perfect silence by the cosmos.

- The glorious moon is right in front of you like a gigantic mirror. You can see your own reflection in the light she reflects from the sun. You can see yourself through all aspects of your life: as a young child, as an adolescent, as a young adult, as a mature adult, as an elder. The images flow smoothly, one into another in a seamless fade so that you can hardly tell when one has begun and another has ended. You realize that the moon is turning, and you are seeing yourself reflected in all the phases: new, waxing gibbous, full, waning gibbous, and new again. As the moon moves through her phases, enacting all aspects of the Triple Goddess, so too are you changing, seeing yourself for the first time against the expanse of time. You realize that you

A Witch's Grimoire

are who you are now, as well as all of the ages you have been and are yet to be.

• You are drawn even closer to the moon until you feel that you are being absorbed into her. Any sense of yourself begins to dissolve as you become integrated with the pure and perfect white light. You feel it permeating every pore of your being. You are pure consciousness living in a brilliant glow of light. The moonlight moves through you. It is you; you are a part of it.

• Take a moment to pause and experience being pure consciousness. Listen to the will of the universe and see your place within the divine matrix.

• Slowly, you begin to pull yourself together back into your familiar form. You feel perfectly at peace. The moon is before you once again; so huge you can see nothing else.

• Slowly, the moon begins to drift back and you are once again able to see it against the backdrop of the night sky. Even the stars seem closer and more familiar.

• You look down and you can see the earth rising up to meet you. You turn back to the moon and it is a little farther away. You feel the familiar atmosphere surround you once again.

• When you look down, you can see the checkered patterns of civilization on the earth, even the pattern of city lights scattered across the land.

• Down, down you descend until you are once again among the familiar tops of the trees. The sounds of crickets and frogs fill your ears with a welcoming melody. You can smell the organic scents of the forest.

Book of Visions

- Slowly, slowly you touch the earth again and find yourself gazing again into the pool, contemplating the reflection of the moon and the reflection of all the lives you have lived on this earth, all of the different people you have become, and all that is still left for you to discover.

- You understand that the nature of change is inherent in life. You can see it with every turn of the tides, with every silver crescent that you know in your heart to be a full circle, even when it is hidden.

- You stand up and gaze into the pool one last time before turning to the path that brought you here. Dried leaves crunch under your feet. The creatures of the night that welcomed you with their song now bid you a fond farewell until you meet again. Even the trees in the grove seem to wave farewell in the night breeze.

- You leave the forest with the bright moonlight casting shadows as you pass. You smile with the knowledge that this sacred grove will always be here for you when you are in need of peaceful contemplation and self-awareness.

- You look up at the moon, now high overhead, seemingly as unattainable as ever (except to astronauts). You think about the journey you have taken tonight. You have bathed in the moonlight and it has touched every part of you. You are a child of the goddess and this light now lives within you to illuminate your path wherever you choose to wander.

Congratulations. You have just taken a trip to the moon. Pause for a moment to focus your thoughts and reacquaint yourself with your "real-life" surroundings. When you are ready, answer the following questions:

A Witch's Grimoire

[?] Were you able to visualize yourself at the edge of the forest? How did you feel before entering the dark woods? Did you experience excitement or trepidation?

_____

_____

_____

_____

_____

[?] Were you able to hear the sounds of the night? How did they make you feel? How long did the path seem to you? Was it a few steps, or was it many miles?

_____

_____

_____

_____

_____

[?] Were you able to visualize the moonlight in the grove? Did the grove seem familiar to you? What was the temperature of the water in the pool? Was it cold or temperate, or warm to the touch?

Book of Visions

[?] How did you feel about leaving the earth? How did you manage to rise above the trees? Did you float or fly? Did you use anything to help you? Any movements (flapping arms), or tools (wings or a broom)?

[?] When you came back down to the earth, was your descent swift or slow? Did you feel as though you were falling, or did you feel as though you were in control of the situation?

By answering these questions honestly and as soon as possible after you complete the visualization, you are training your mind to imagine specific details regarding fantastic situations and recall them accurately. This will aid you in the work to come, whether it is casting spells or recording prophetic dreams.

The Chakras

Just as a creative visualization can be done within the space of an hour or so to get you more in tune with your spiritual nature, so too can you open up your psychic center by energizing and balancing your chakras. Just as the physical body has internal organs that enable it to function and perform various tasks necessary for survival, the astral body has "organs" of its own that also need attention. There are seven major chakras in all, each one with a different corresponding function and color, each one a separate spiraling center of energy. Think of the chakras as aspects of your aura, the energy that your spirit transmits to others. To many, the auras and chakras are visible, and modern technology even makes the photography of auras possible.

Within the energy body that surrounds and emanates from our physical body is the chakra system. When our chakras are in balance, our intuitive and psychic abilities are at their strongest. When you balance your chakras, you are preparing yourself to receive divine inspiration and energy. But if you don't balance your chakra system, it is very likely that you will be unprepared for many of the magical workings you try. Preparing an altar or other sacred space while neglecting to thoroughly prepare yourself can lead to failure as, instead of being energized and inspired, you may find yourself

Book of Visions

drained and exhausted. It is not uncommon for people who are unprepared to experience confusion and even distress if they attempt a ritual beyond their readiness and comprehension. No other preparation will compare with the time you spend developing yourself.

The divine essence of all the chakras is *kundalini*. Kundalini manifests symbolically as a serpent coiled around herself three and a half times. She sleeps at the base of the spine and awakens with a rattle or a hiss. She slowly uncoils herself and begins her ascent, traveling through each chakra center, opening and activating it as she goes. Each major chakra has a different significant symbol, though all are variations of the lotus flower. Use the symbols as a guide to understanding and integrating these energies so that you may experience the benefits. Any visual aid that enables you to mentally connect with a concept increases understanding and acceptance of that concept.

THE ROOT CHAKRA

The root chakra is located at the base of the spine. Its color is red. The root chakra deals with all issues pertaining to survival and surrounding environmental influences. It can encompass your actual physical survival as well as the survival of your soul. Here is where many of your fight-or-flight responses and animal instincts are stored. To open the root chakra is to embrace your primal being as an integrated and necessary part of your higher self. If you cannot survive, you will never thrive.

In addition to survival in the literal sense, this chakra also impacts how you interact with the world. The root chakra is concerned with your sense of self and your confidence. If your root chakra is balanced, you are likely to feel secure about your place in the world and your ability to cope with any hardships that may come your way. Blockages in the root chakra may lead to feelings of inadequacy and insecurity, and a lack of confidence with one's place in the world.

Because you may find that your beliefs will often be challenged by mainstream society, a strong sense of self is a necessary quality in one who practices Wicca. You can strengthen your root chakra by meditating and directing your energy to the base of your spine while envisioning a glowing red ball of energy spinning and growing brighter and stronger. Visual aids are a great asset to meditation, and you can use the lotus flower as a guide to envisioning the opening of the root chakra. The root chakra is your connection to the earth. Strengthening this connection will help solidify your relationship to the Goddess.

THE SACRAL CHAKRA

The sacral chakra is located just below the navel. Its color is orange. The sacral chakra deals with issues of sexuality, desire, attraction, and fulfillment. Here is the realm of procreation and pleasure, where all of your carnal instincts reside. To open your sacral chakra is to embrace yourself as a sexual being and to accept pleasure. It is to view the act of sex as a purely natural and sacred function of the universe, without which human and animal life would not endure.

In addition to the correlation with sexuality, the sacral chakra impacts other kinds of desire as well. Hopes and dreams and aspirations for the future dwell here, as do those entities that we wish to call unto ourselves. Connecting with the sacral chakra is necessary to understanding the Wiccan Charge of the Goddess, where the Goddess states through her priestess: "All acts of love and pleasure are mine."

The act of spell casting represents the intention of having a specific need or desire fulfilled through direct action that is carried out to bring about the desired outcome.

If your sacral chakra is in balance, you are likely to feel comfortable with your sexuality and be adept at understanding and stating your own needs on many levels, as well as seeing that these needs are met. A deficiency in the sacral chakra may lead to feelings of discomfort regarding sexuality and difficulty expressing requirements for fulfillment in other aspects of life. A sense of pleasure and comfort may be superseded by feelings of longing and repression. Balancing your sacral chakra will help assuage any residual feelings of guilt or embarrassment, even pain that may be connected to sexual issues. A balanced sacral chakra will also lead you to more effective spell casting because you will gain greater comfort with your own needs and the ability to express them clearly and effectively to bring about the changes that you desire. Meditate on the opening of the lotus flower as you visualize the spinning vortex of energy glowing a bright orange just below your navel. As you activate your sacral chakra, you will feel the kundalini energy start to rise and enhance your magical work.

THE SOLAR PLEXUS CHAKRA

The chakra that governs the strength of your will is located in the solar plexus, just above your navel. Its color is yellow. Here is where you actualize your ego and your personal gifts and talents. This is the place where your personal power resides. To open your solar plexus chakra is to take responsibility for your choices and determine your unique place in the universe. Engaging this chakra can be highly empowering, for it becomes a necessary foundation for activating the higher functions.

Think of each chakra as building upon the previous chakra. Once you have experienced the balance of energy from the root and the sacral chakra, your confidence is higher and you are adept at stating your needs. The bright yellow sun of the solar plexus chakra will assist you in making an impact on the world around you by putting you in touch with the ability to use your unique talents to manifest positive results for your own benefit and the benefit of others. Think of the power of your inner sun radiating outward to touch all beings. Being in harmony with yourself and with others will allow you to open the gateway to the higher functions of the self, and to recognize yourself as a unique and individual sacred being. Your personal talents will come to fruition, which will bring you a greater sense of self-worth and attainment.

THE HEART CHAKRA

The heart chakra is located in the middle of the chest. Its color is green. This chakra deals with all issues pertaining to the heart and your ability to love and be loved. The heart chakra is the link between your physical body and your spiritual identity; it is through this gateway that the path of love travels. The heart chakra represents the love of self and the love of community, be it family, friends, or humanity at large. The heart chakra is also our connection to love of nature and the ethereal spirits that we recognize and accept as integral parts of the spiritual domain. It is love without fear, embracing the interconnections that all creatures, human, animal, plant, and mineral, share in accordance with the divine will of the universe. To open your heart chakra is to experience love without walls, to transcend the fear of being hurt, to accept one's own vulnerability, and to show constant faith in the face of the unknown.

Blockages in the heart chakra can lead to feelings of unworthiness, mistrust, and loneliness. People who have had their hearts broken often distance themselves from the heart chakra by affirming isolating philosophies, such as "I will never allow anyone to get that close to me again," or "No one will ever get the chance to hurt me like that again." Remember, it is often through the pain and disappointment of loss of love that our compassion is activated. Through compassion, we learn to recognize our similarity to all beings.

To open your heart chakra, meditate on the green petals of the lotus as they unfold within the spiraling center of glowing light, opening slowly and growing larger, sending forth love and reception to love as well. Remember that green is the color of healing, also of growth. With growth, however, there is often pain. While unavoidable in life, pain is still a great teacher. Allow yourself to learn from your experiences and learn to heal yourself from them as well. Learn to accept healing and understand when it is time to tear down and give up the barriers to your heart so that you may fully experience the divine love, which is the law that binds the universe.

THE THROAT CHAKRA

The throat chakra is located—appropriately—at the throat. Its color is light blue. The throat chakra deals with all matters of communication and how you interact with others in the world around you and within the higher planes of consciousness. The throat chakra is also the domain of spiritual communication and psychic gifts. The manner by which you formulate and verbalize your thoughts is affected by the throat chakra.

The fifth chakra is distinct from the preceding four in that it is the first chakra across the bridge into the purely spiritual realm. While all of the main chakras are considered integral parts of the astral body, the first four chakras have distinct correlations with parts of the physical body as well. The base of the spine, the sex organs, the solar plexus, and the heart are all recognizable physical entities, whereas the third eye and the crown are more metaphysical concepts. The throat chakra is the gateway between these two aspects of the astral body; it is still connected to a recognizable physical entity as well as the spiritual plane. The throat chakra is the center that allows you to accept the inspiration of an oracle and integrate and verbalize it, then convey the message to others. People who have effectively attuned their throat chakras are comfortable talking about spiritual experiences and may even feel compelled to do so. The fifth chakra allows us to accept messages from the spiritual realm just as easily as we might accept a message on an answering machine.

Imbalance of the throat chakra can manifest as an overly dogmatic approach to interpreting spiritual messages or excessive talkativeness without listening. Listening is perhaps the single most important ingredient in communication. People with an unbalanced throat chakra may have difficulty listening or interpreting the messages that they receive, which can lead to conflict.

To enhance your fifth chakra, imagine the lotus just in front of your throat. Every word you speak passes through it, passes through its beautiful blue light, akin to the sky on a bright and cloudless day. Everything that passes through the petals of the lotus is bathed in the serene blue light of highest clarity. Perhaps for the first time in your life, you stand on the brink of being truly understood. When your throat chakra is activated and in balance, there is no chance for miscommunication or misunderstanding. You accept yourself as a spiritual being. You release all skepticism and pessimism. You are able to let divine energy flow through you, and you are able to learn from its timeless wisdom.

THE THIRD EYE CHAKRA

The third eye chakra is located in the forehead. Its color is indigo. This is the chakra of psychic awareness. All matters pertaining to your intuition and your relationship to the divine spirit reside here. The sixth major chakra symbolizes the release of all that is mundane, all of the phantasmagoric distractions that we are so often tempted to define as reality. It represents the perfect balance of masculine and feminine energies and the transcendence of individual identity. This is not to say that the identity is completely abandoned; rather it is seen as merely a facet of the greater spiritual nature. The sixth chakra allows you to experience your spiritual nature through manifestations like clairvoyance (seeing the unseen), memories of past lives, and empathy (actually feeling what others feel), telepathy (getting clear and unmistakable access to the thoughts of another), and astral travel (where the spirit enters realms the physical body cannot). People who have activated their third eye chakras will often be drawn to and be quite comfortable with the occult.

People with an imbalance of the sixth chakra may use its power to achieve selfish ends. They may become obsessed with their own abilities and demand the status of a spiritual teacher or guru when it is not necessarily deserved. A block in the sixth chakra can lead someone to reject his or her own psychic gifts out of fear or revulsion.

To activate your sixth chakra, picture the deep blue indigo light emanating from your third eye. All of your thoughts pass through this gate of mystery, and your thoughts are brought into equilibrium by the two lotus petals that unfold in perfect graceful harmony. Your walls and masks fall away and your true spiritual nature is revealed. You now recognize yourself as an integral facet of the divine essence. Your connection to the Goddess has never been clearer. Gone are the old patterns of skepticism and doubt. Gone is the desire to cling to useless programming. You arise anew as the true reflection of your higher self.

THE CROWN CHAKRA

The crown chakra is located at or just above the top of the head. Its color is purple, though some see it as white. The crown chakra deals with the ultimate realization of the higher self as a fully integrated aspect of the divine reality. All spiritual matters pertaining to your soul's existence dwell here. Separation between the identity of self as individual or spirit disappears. When you activate your crown chakra, your ego completely falls away and you live in a state of absolute acceptance and assimilation with the divine. All of your needs are met. You are in a place beyond desire. Communication is effortless and instantaneous. The spirit flows through you, becomes you, and you are inextricably bound in a blissful spiritual union, at peace with all creatures, in love with the universe without any boundary or separation between yourself and the goddess. You experience a sense of oneness with all beings. You are at the center of the lotus with a thousand petals that extend outward to touch all things. You are in the constant presence of the divine with complete access to its mysteries. You fear nothing, not even death.

An imbalance in the crown chakra can manifest as appearing utterly lost in your own world or suffering from apparent delusions of grandeur.

To bring your seventh chakra into balance, meditate on the lotus with a thousand petals. Each petal is an aspect of the Goddess, yet all are one. Allow yourself to visualize a brilliant, regal purple light emanating from the top of your head, flowing over you and through you. The lotus unfolds the thousand petals. You remain at the center, surrounded by the love of the

Goddess as her mysteries become known to you. You are a part of her, as she is a part of you, and you are one. You carry this gift with you forever, no matter where your journeys may take you.

Meditation

Meditation is an effective method of relaxing the body and opening the mind. The purpose of a meditation is to quiet the mind. This releases the din our minds are normally subjected to. You will also gain deeper listening skills so that spiritual and psychic messages can be received and interpreted. A daily meditation practice is very useful. It will enable you to build upon the work you have done and to have better access to your creative mind, which will enhance your writing or other work you do. Any routine that is regularly adhered to becomes a ritual and should be recognized as such.

Experiment with different meditation techniques and make them a part of your spiritual practice. Find the one that is the most productive for the results that you desire.

THE CYCLE OF BREATH

Begin by finding a comfortable sitting position. It is important to clear your physical space of distractions that will inhibit your meditation; after all, you are trying to achieve a peaceful and relaxed state of consciousness. A ringing telephone can be an interruption that can ruin your session. Any other distractions should be dealt with before you begin.

Once you have achieved a comfortable position, pay attention to how your body feels. Make sure you're sitting in a position that you will be able to maintain for some time. If you get the sensation that your feet are falling asleep, you will need to shift around until you're comfortable. Many people find that sitting cross-legged on the floor works well, though others cannot tolerate this position at all. Some are able to maintain the lotus position, in which one sits cross-legged on the floor with the feet tucked over the thighs, hands resting on the thighs and palms facing upward, sometimes with the thumb and index finger touching. You may even experiment with lying down, but remember that the purpose of meditation is relaxing the body and opening the mind, and not falling asleep. While comfort is important, you do not want to be so comfortable that you lose interest in the meditation and end up snoozing. Maintaining both focus and relaxation is an important aspect of developing a meditative practice.

Once you have achieved a comfortable and sustainable position, sit with your spine as straight as possible. Imagine a silver cord rising from the top of your head, pulling you up toward the sky. This image will help you maintain proper spinal alignment. Also envision a cord extending from the base of your spine deep into the earth. This will help keep you grounded. Sitting with your spine very straight also helps you retain your energy, for when you slouch over, your internal organs are crowded on top of one another and cannot perform at their most efficient level of function. Such a lack of alignment is not an optimal position for maintaining an energized state of being. What you are seeking is a relaxed, but invigorated state. You feel calm and at peace, but alive and very much full of energy.

1. Begin by taking very deep breaths. Establish a cycle of breathing by inhaling to a count of three and then exhaling to a count of three.

2. Repeat this cycle of breathing for nine repetitions. Once you have done the nine repetitions, increase the length of time you spend inhaling and exhaling.

3. You can add one additional count and repeat this cycle three times. Add another count, again repeating it until you have achieved what feels to be your utmost lung capacity. Breathing at your fullest capacity increases oxygen levels in your brain and in your blood, thus touching every part of

your body. The oxygen blast you are giving yourself is purifying. It will unleash your creativity and keep your mind and body in good working order.

Focus only on the breathing at first. When the cycle feels natural to you and is no longer an effort, it is time to continue with your chosen technique of meditation.

BREATH OF FIRE

Air is the sustenance that gives fire its life. As you did in the air meditation on pages 26–28, begin your breathing sequence by focusing on the cycle of energy released and replenished. As you breathe with the intention of creating a relaxed state of being and an energized state of mind, you are in fact performing an act of transformation. Breath becomes life and life becomes breath.

1. Inhale through your nose to your fullest lung capacity. Hold the breath for a count of three and then exhale in short, managed bursts, using the syllable "kh" with each exhalation. When you get to the end of exhaling your lung capacity, release any remaining air in your lungs by blowing out through your mouth.

2. Repeat this three times and then pause for a moment to observe how your perception has changed. If you are experiencing a feeling of lightheadedness, go back to focusing on the slow deep breathing exercise described before, and then proceed slowly with the breath of fire technique.

Touch Sound

The preceding techniques have focused on breathing in silence to bring about a tranquil and receptive state of mind. The element of sound can be a great asset to meditation.

Book of Visions

1. Resume a comfortable position. Tap into your cycle of breath.

2. Focus on listening to the environment around you. Make mental notes of the things you hear, however faint or seemingly inconsequential they may be. Allow the sounds to merge into an indiscernible primal sound, a sound that is difficult to categorize.

3. Let your mind create the humming of an air conditioner. Let this hum become the humming vibration of a planet traveling through space. Let the sounds of distant chatter meld into the whisperings of the spirit.

4. Continue to breathe and as you listen carefully to all of the sounds around you, make a low, nonverbal sound as you exhale.

5. Continue to breathe, releasing a sound on every exhalation, each time allowing the sound to grow louder and stronger. But do not force it. Release your inhibitions and love the sound of your own voice.

6. Get into a repetitious cycle of transforming air into breath, breath into life, and life into the vibration of sound.

7. Continue developing the sound until it takes a distinct and repeatable form. You are creating your own mantra, the primal vibration that links us with the spiritual world. The best-known mantra is the Sanskrit word "OM," pronounced *ohm*. You can use this sound or create a unique vibration of your own. The mantra is the primal sound of the universe that connects us to the past and the future. It is in a place beyond formal language; it is the language of the spirit.

8. In addition to creating your own vibration through vocalization, you may also use the sound produced by striking a bell. Strike the bell

deliberately and focus on the sound in its entirety as you breathe. Experience every aspect of the vibration, from its actualization that pierces the silence and awakens the mind, to the sustain that carries it through the air, to the gentle fade as it dissipates into the ether.

9. Let the sound disappear completely and meditate in a moment of silence before striking the bell again. As you listen to the cycle of sound, imagine that you are listening to the voice of the Goddess. She carries a special message for you. Keep your mind tranquil and open so that you may receive the blessings of her divine presence.

Take some time to answer the following questions so that you can better understand the benefits of meditation.

[?] Were you able to release your daily cares and enter a state of mental tranquility, or did you find yourself distracted? If the meditation was difficult, what was it that distracted you? If you found it easy, what tools or visualizations did you use to quiet the mind?

_____

_____

_____

_____

_____

Book of Visions

[?] As you practiced the Breath of Fire, on the average, about how many short exhalations were you able to sustain? Did you find yourself feeling winded or energized? Was this technique difficult for you? What do you think you can do to maximize its effectiveness?

_____

_____

_____

_____

_____

[?] Did your meditation benefit from using a mantra? Is there a mantra that you are already comfortable with? Were you inspired to create your own? What kinds of sounds did you hear when you opened yourself to pure listening?

_____

_____

_____

_____

_____

5

Book of Days

You have spent much time exploring the proper environment for casting a spell, conjuring a charm, or enacting a ritual. Now an important part of your preparation must include choosing an auspicious day that will empower your intentions and give the work its fullest effectiveness. Different days have different aspects and some days are better suited to specific types of work than others. Always consult your calendar before committing to a ritual. Perhaps you are planning something for a certain day, and the influences of that particular day seem out of alignment with the work you intend to do. You shouldn't necessarily forbid yourself from performing a spell due to a certain day of the week, but plan with the knowledge of what you are up against. Realize that there are extant forces in the environment that will have an effect on the outcome, and the more you familiarize yourself with these influences, the better you will be able to use them to your advantage.

Each day has a rich pagan history of its own, and most days are named for ancient Nordic deities. Each day of the week also has a planetary influence.

Sunday

Sunday is traditionally the first day of the week on the Western calendar. As suggested by its name, Sunday is ruled by the sun. This makes it a desirable day for any magical work that involves growth, family, community, inspiration, and identifying with the aspects of the God. Because Sunday is conducive to bringing people together, it is an excellent day for performing group ritual. With its biblical connotation of being a day of rest, the day is also suited for solitary meditation and introspection. Meditate on the aspects of the sun gods like Ra (Egyptian) or Apollo (Greek) to lend strength and meaning to your work.

{ ? } Write down three ideas for spells that you would like to create that would be significant on a Sunday.

_____

_____

_____

Monday

Monday is ruled by the moon. Magical work planned for a Monday should involve aspects of the Goddess and any rites to honor her. In Wicca, the phases of the moon are revered as natural symbols of the different phases of womanhood. Spells and rituals invoking change are appropriate for a Monday.

Book of Days

The moon rules the tides, so spells involving water are also appropriate for this time. Think of purification and cleansing work that you may need to do. Even consecrating your chalice would be an appropriate work for a Monday. Meditate on the aspects of the Greek maiden huntress, Artemis, twin sister of Apollo, or on her Roman counterpart, Diana of the silver bow. The lunar energy will bless your work if you acknowledge it correctly.

{ ? } Write down three ideas for lunar magic spells that you would like to create.

_____

_____

_____

Tuesday

Tuesday is ruled by the planet Mars and named for the Nordic god Tyr, the invincible warrior whose attributes are strength, attainment of desire, and manifestation of the will. Spells and rituals in alignment with Tuesday would be those involving conflict resolution or competition. Mars is also the god of war in the Roman pantheon, and while this does not mean that violence and chaos will occur on Tuesdays, it should be taken into account that this day is better suited for strategic planning or defensive maneuvers.

Perhaps you have the strong sense that you have been a victim of a psychic attack from another person. Tuesday would be a good day to practice a reversing spell so that no further harm may come to you. It is also a good time to build your psychic defenses through protection rituals. Meditate on the end of conflict and the return of peace.

A Witch's Grimoire

{ ? } Write down three ideas for spells that would be appropriate to enact on a Tuesday.

_____

_____

_____

Wednesday

Wednesday is ruled by the planet Mercury and named for the Norse god Woden, or Odin. Odin is the father of the gods and represents ultimate wisdom. In Roman mythology, Mercury is the messenger of the gods and is often viewed as an aspect of Odin; both deities are characterized as wanderers with sharp wits.

Rites and spells for Wednesday involve communication and the sending and receiving of messages. Developing your attunement to goddesses and gods to receive an oracular communication would be a desirable effort for a Wednesday divination. Work involving communication with spirits, with a pendulum, runes, or some other tool with which you have some expertise would be suitable as well. Writers, poets, and scholars will also benefit from the influences of this day.

{ ? } Write down three ideas for spells that would benefit from being performed on a Wednesday.

_____

_____

_____

Book of Days

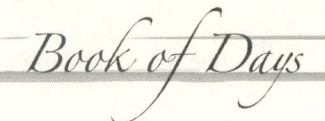

Thursday

Thursday is ruled by the planet Jupiter, the Roman king of the gods, and is named for the god Thor. Political and legal issues are appropriate themes for the spells and rituals of this day, as are rites of abundance and material success. Thor is the thunder bearer and wields a mighty hammer, signifying strength and victory. If you are trying to influence the outcome of a legal proceeding, you may find that enacting the spell on a Thursday will be advantageous to you. Perhaps you have strong political allegiances and wish to make a difference in an electoral proceeding. You may find that working your magic on a Thursday gives it an added significance. Perhaps you have been trying to call to yourself the ideal employment situation, or maybe you are in need of a financial windfall. Lighting a green candle on Thursday will improve the effectiveness of your endeavors.

[?] Write down ideas for three spells that would benefit from the energy of a Thursday.

_____

_____

_____

Friday

Friday is dedicated to the planet Venus, personified as the Roman goddess of love. The Nordic goddess Freya, the patroness of women of power, gave her name to this day. In Norse mythology, she presides over the Valkyries, the winged goddesses who bring fallen heroes to Valhalla, the realm of the gods. Renowned for her beauty, Freya is often called "the Fair One." Any spells or charms relating to matters of the heart are appropriate for this day, as well as divination for inspiration in the arts. The influence of Venus is strong on Fridays and makes this day suitable for issues dealing with love, comfort, and the fulfillment of desire.

[?] Write down three ideas for spells that would be appropriate for a Friday.

_____

_____

_____

Saturday

Saturday is ruled by the planet Saturn, who represents ultimate mystery. Any rituals dealing with occult knowledge, the unknown, transformation, even death, are appropriate for a Saturday. Saturn is also the planet of karma, so any work dealing with past life regressions or karmic lessons would be advantageous on this day.

[?] Write down ideas for three spells or divinations that could be performed on a Saturday.

_____

_____

_____

Book of Days

Morning Rites

Part of your morning routine should be writing in your book of shadows as soon as you awaken. This way, the images from your dreams will be fresh and you will not be challenged later when you forget an elusive detail. In addition to your writing, you may want to come up with a simple ritual that will color the rest of your day. Anything that you do every day with awareness is a ritual, whether it's a brisk shower or a morning cup of coffee. The challenge is to make the ritual sacred to receive the benefits of divine grace. You may only need a few moments of time to transform your morning experience to lead you to a more inspired and productive day.

1. You may begin by setting your altar with a small stone, a cup or chalice of water, a bit of incense, and an essential oil that you find pleasing. Take a moment to reflect before your altar in silence and think about the types of energies that you would like to call to yourself to influence the unfolding day. Imagine your perfect day and try to form a very clear image of it in your mind. You may have a specific accomplishment in mind, or perhaps there is a new and beneficial habit you have been wanting to adopt but are procrastinating about. Picture yourself in a state of attainment. See yourself achieving what your heart desires. Imagine yourself doing all of the "I meant to's" in a state of joy and satisfaction. When the image of what you want is clear, speak the following words aloud, or improvise your own:

> *Rosy-fingered Eos, goddess of the dawn who paints the morning sky with light*
> *I ask for your blessing and rejoice as you set the sky alight.*
> *I anoint myself as your child, alive and anew with your radiant energy.*

A Witch's Grimoire

2. Take your vial of oil and place a small drop on your fingertip. Touch your fingertip to your third eye. See yourself bathed in the light of the breaking dawn.

3. Light the incense and let its perfume waft over you. Take in its aroma and speak the following words:

The fires of day have risen. Let my heart's desire rise up to the feet of the Goddess, that she may gather and direct my sacred intention with her wisdom and power. As the sun climbs through the sky, bless me, Lady of the Morning, who bestows all abundance to her devotees. So mote it be.

4. Take the cup of water and hold it aloft to greet the day. Bring it down to chest level, close to your heart. Dip your fingers in the water, close your eyes, and place a little water on each eyelid.

Beautiful Iris, who adorns the sky with rainbows of light, bring me clarity of vision and bless my sight that I may see the true nature of those around me. May I be blessed in your eyes.

5. Take the stone and hold it in your hands, feeling it come alive with your energy. Imbue the stone with the intentions of what you would most like to manifest on this day. As you hold the stone, speak the following words or improvise your own.

Blessed earth, blessed by the dawn, I honor you and your unending grace. May my existence be blessed with your sacred treasure. May I share the abundance of the Goddess on this day.

Book of Days

You may carry the stone around with you as a talisman to aid in maintaining your focus throughout the day. You can also personalize the preceding rite by using other goddess names.

[?] Write down your ideas for a personal and specific morning rite, based on the simple outline provided above.

_____

_____

_____

_____

_____

Evening Rites

Twilight is an utterly magical time. The sun sinks low in the horizon, coloring the sky with a brilliance rivaled only by the dawn. Behind the setting sun, darkness approaches in indigo hues, succumbing to violet, and finally to blackness. There is no time of day that makes us feel more attuned to the concept of "between the worlds." Neither the light of day nor the dark of night holds sway. This is the time of transition when the reality of daylight melds with the mysteries of darkness. This magical time can be celebrated simply and beautifully with a well-crafted evening rite.

1. Begin by reflecting on the day that has just passed. Contemplate the energies you have experienced, which things went as you had hoped and which things you would like to have changed if given the chance.

A Witch's Grimoire

2. Place a cup of water and a stone on your altar. Light some incense, light a candle. Invoke the mysteries of the night with this charge:

Queen of the night, radiant goddess who shines forth in her many aspects through the myriad of stars, bless this coming darkness. I ask for your blessing as a devotee who seeks to honor you and learn your great mysteries.

3. Hold the incense aloft and say:

As the curling whispers of smoke rise to greet the night sky, so does my mind rise along the rivers of dreamtime to welcome you, beloved Goddess, into my dreams. I invoke you and I invite you to inspire my dreams that I may experience your divine grace.

4. Light the candle and meditate on its softly glowing flame. Use these words or improvise your own:

I step between the worlds into a world both in and out of time. The candle lights my path as the moon lights the night sky. I gaze upon your great beauty in wonder, Goddess of the ages, Lady of mystery, thou who art brighter than all the stars.

5. Hold your cup or chalice and take a sip of water:

May your abundance flow through me, may dreams and visions come to me. May the unseen be seen and the power of sight granted to me that I may perceive in the night that which is unknowable by day.

Book of Days

6. Pick up your stone and hold it to your third eye:

Rare gem of the night, send forth your light to guide me through the darkness. I enter into your starry realm in love and trust, abandoning all fear with the knowledge that you are with me ever, in my thoughts and in my dreams as I do not merely sleep, but awaken to your presence.

As in the morning rite, you may substitute the specific name of a particular goddess to whom you are devoted.

[?] Think about what you would like to glean from your dreams. Inspiration? Prophecy? Self-knowledge? Take a few minutes to write down your ideas and craft them into an original evening rite to add to your grimoire.

_____

_____

_____

_____

_____

Dreamwork

In the dark of night, thoughts begin to take form and significance. Shimmering dreams materialize into energy that is experienced through the senses, seeming to emanate from an unknowable source. We call this source *imagination* and we recognize that its origin lies in the unconscious mind. Some of the greatest moments of inspiration occur while we are sleeping.

When traveling the river of dreamtime, the mind is unbound, uncensored, and released from expectation. Images, whether comforting or frightening, flow freely in an endless succession of vivid possibilities. We may dream about something, and, waking, find evidence of its existence in our "real world." Dreams often contain prophecy and can be full of portent and premonition. Too often, we come into consciousness from lucidity with the thought, "What an amazing dream, I will have to write that one down later." Then we find that we become engrossed in the mundane activities of life, and the subtle nuances of inspiration we received while dreaming are gone forever. Fortunately, there are techniques that can be used to call upon the magic of dreams when we are most in need of their influence.

To get the most out of recording your dreams, start writing them down immediately upon waking. You will be better able to capture the fleeting images before they vanish into the ether if you keep your book of shadows and a pen or pencil close at hand. It is not important to write in complete sentences. It is only important that you write first upon awakening: before you contemplate that cup of coffee, before you select your wardrobe for the day, before you begin any other aspect of your morning ritual.

This may seem unproductive at first. You may feel groggy and inarticulate from sleep. Take heart. This is precisely the point! You do not want your brain fully engaged; you are trying to capture the images and symbols that occur first to the unconscious mind. You are not trying to rationalize, explain, or even understand your thought process at this point. You are merely recording it.

Try a stream of consciousness approach to writing and do not worry about sentence structure or narrative. Let the images flow freely. Try to capture on paper what occurs so easily to your dreaming mind.

Do not place any value judgments on what you write. Do not say your writing is good, bad, mediocre, interesting, or boring. As long as you are recording your dreams and thoughts honestly, without the imposition of rationality, you are doing just fine. Keep in mind that as we dream, we tap into a universal consciousness. Dream images have been shown to recur all over the world, regardless of country of origin, age, or culture of the dreamers.

As a part of your evening rite, you may want to write a few lines about your day in your grimoire. Oftentimes, dreams will occur in response to a circumstance, person, or event encountered during waking hours. Record the significance of any encounter or event that transpired during the day and your emotional response to the situation. This will help you when you move into dream interpretation.

Record Your Dreams

When you begin to write about a dream, your writing may seem as disjointed and unusual as the dream itself. Remember, you are just trying to record the dominant images, obvious symbols, or other events that occurred to your dreaming mind. Interpretation will come later, after you have had a chance to examine the complexities of what your mind can create.

Try giving your dream a title that relates to what you remember as the most vivid or distinct image. The title could reflect the strongest event that occurred, the main action that the events of the dream revolved around.

Once you have given your dream a title, you can begin to look for some sort of structure in your dream. Many dreams have no apparent structure at all, but some do. If your dream contains any identifiable plotline, try to break it down in the following manner. First, identify the *situation*, the "what" of the dream. Write down what is happening, around you, to you, because of you. These circumstances, which may be within or outside the realm of your control, are the outer framework that is the foundation of the specific details of your dream. Next, look for the *crossroads*, or the point in the dream at which things began to change, either for positive or negative results. A crossroad is any significant interruption of the main action of the dream. This is where

A Witch's Grimoire

dreams spiral up or down, either into delightful pleasure or nightmare. This turn in action could be a distinctly recognizable event or the appearance of a person or entity. Finally, try to pinpoint some sort of *resolution* to the situation or main action and the crossroad, or conflict. Recognizing these three dream components will assist you in unlocking the secrets of your dream imagery.

Later in the day, when your thoughts are better organized, you can build on the recorded essence of your dreams to better understand them by listing the main action, identifiable theme, or central image of the dream. Following the central theme, make a list of all your personal associations with the subject. They may range from childhood memories to recent encounters. Try to think about the image of your dream out of the context of the dream to see what other associations you have with that particular subject matter. Last, try to identify your cultural and subcultural associations with the image. These associations will most likely be influenced by your upbringing, traditions you observe, knowledge gained through learning, television shows you have been exposed to, world events, movies, or anything else that you have been witness to throughout your life.

Keeping records of your dreams will lead you to a better understanding of your unconscious mind. It is the power of the mind that we seek to activate when we practice magic. Keep a section of your grimoire dedicated to dreamwork, and you will find that you are growing more adept at recognizing, identifying, and interpreting symbols and imagery. Once you have attained proficiency with documenting your dreams, you will be able to invite desirable and mystic awakening into your dreaming mind.

The Temple Sleep

Dreams allow us to explore what lies beneath the surface, the unspoken world of image and mystery that lies dormant, ready to rise and make its presence known in our lives. The Goddess may come to you in dreams through symbols and signs. She travels from a place beyond, both in and out of time. Enter into her temple with the intention to know her and to open your unconscious mind to her presence, her words, and her teachings.

Let the room be dark, except for a lighted candle or two, but no more. Lie flat on your back with your head pointing north, preferably toward your altar as well. Relax and get comfortable. You will be here for a while. Visualize yourself approaching the doorway of a grand temple. You walk up the wide marble steps between two towering columns. Inside, the walls are illuminated by the fiery dance of torch sconces. Flowers adorn the high altar and curls of fragrant incense waft through the air.

1. Begin by focusing on rhythmic breathing. Inhale, and energy is transformed from air into breath. Exhale, and energy is released back into the atmosphere from whence it came, forever changed by you.

2. Continue this rhythmic breathing until it is well established. You should feel relaxed, but invigorated with energy flowing through you, as in a successful meditation.

3. Inhale, and tighten all of your facial muscles in a deliberate grimace. Exhale, and relax them, assuming your usual countenance.

4. Inhale and tighten your shoulders, bringing them up toward your ears.

5. Exhale and release the tension, allowing your shoulders to drop to their normal position. Inhale and clench your fists tightly. As you breathe out, let your hands relax and go limp.

6. On your next intake of breath, arch your back and neck as much as you can without straining. Think of trying to look at the north altar that is just beyond your head. Hold this pose for a moment; exhale and relax your spine.

7. As you inhale, tighten the muscles in your buttocks. Exhale and release the tension. Inhale and tighten your thigh muscles. Exhale and release. Inhale and flex your feet, even curling your toes. Exhale and relax your legs. Lie still for a moment and notice the change in your energy.

8. Continue the steady, rhythmic breathing and begin to visualize a soft, red, glowing pinpoint of light located at the very base of your spine. As you breathe, allow your vision of this light to grow so that the pinpoint grows first brighter, then larger, as it envelops your entire body in a warm, red aura, surrounding you and comforting you. Just as slowly as the light grew to surround you, allow it to collapse within itself and return to the pinpoint at the base of your spine where it began.

9. Continue your cycle of breathing and begin to visualize a tiny pinpoint of orange light emanating from just below your navel. As you did before, focus on the pinpoint of orange light, allowing it to grow in size and in intensity until it covers your entire being in a warm blanket of peace and pleasure. Breathe into this orange light, allowing it to flow through you. Slowly gather the light and send it back to its source until it once again resembles the glowing pinpoint.

10. Sustain your rhythm of breath and envision a pinpoint of yellow light glowing in your solar plexus. The yellow light grows and covers you like a kiss from the sun. You are surrounded by its beauty. Breathe into it, allowing it to grow and permeate every cell in your body. The light extends above you and below you, surrounding you completely. It is a part of you

and you are a part of it. You are inseparable until, by the force of your will, you encourage the light to collapse within itself and return to the pinpoint of light, small but glowing steadily in your solar plexus.

11. As you continue to breathe, you feel your heart open to reveal a pinpoint of bright green light, shiny as a new leaf. The light grows and surrounds you with an overwhelming sense of healing and love. You are covered in green, like a virgin field in the newness of spring. The sensation of pure love flows through you, emanating from your heart but extending outward to touch every part of you, even that which lies beyond your reach. You are whole. You are at peace. You revel in this delightful green aura until you decide to let the green light return to its home, where it continues to thrive as a tiny pinpoint of light nestled safe within your heart.

12. You continue your cycle of rhythmic breathing as you imagine a pinpoint of vivid blue light emanating from your throat. The light grows to surround you with coolness and truth. You breathe into the blue light as though you are floating on an azure sea, buffeted by soothing waves. Enclosed within the radiant blue, you allow yourself to drift into a realm of peace and understanding. You are on the cusp of uncovering a great secret, an ancient wisdom. You wish to travel further, but in order to do so you must first send the radiant blue light back to its origin, where it will continue to glow.

13. You continue to breathe as you envision a deep indigo light glowing in a pinpoint on your forehead right between your eyes. The light grows and its intensity deepens. You are surrounded in the calm of this deep dark indigo. Unseen worlds begin to reveal themselves to you. You are opening your psychic sight. All the work you have done begins to make itself apparent. Knowledge and wisdom inhabit this light, which fills your very being. Breathe slowly and accept the teachings of this light.

14. Breathe gently and allow yourself to be cradled in the light of wisdom. Proceed with your cycle of breath and allow the light to return to your third eye, where it will continue to extend gentle radiance throughout the long night.

15. A tiny pinpoint of purple light begins to emanate from the top of your head. It begins to extend outward like a crown. The light grows until you are surrounded by a regal purple aura.

16. You are covered in this splendor and are experiencing sensations that occur rarely in a lifetime. You are activating your spiritual self, exploring your identity as part of the divine matrix. You are unique and individual, but an aspect of the living Goddess as well.

17. Breathe into this and experience yourself in your highest form and function. You are in a place beyond time and space, able to see the unseen and touch things far beyond your reach.

18. Experience these sensations as ultimate reality. You have chosen this spiritual path, and now your eternal essence is making itself known to you in a very real way. You are experiencing it through this purple light that envelops you totally. You live through this light, and as it extends outward, so do your energy and your essence. Breathe into this light. You will always be a part of it, even as you send it back to its source. It will forever live inside your mind, able to spring forth from your crown whenever you have need of it. You have seen yourself as a pure spiritual being. You have caught a glimpse of your divine essence.

19. Lie still. All along your body are gentle pinpoints of brilliance, bathing you in the colors of the rainbow. You have a sense of completeness and wholeness about you. You are utterly relaxed and at peace. Your mind is

Book of Days

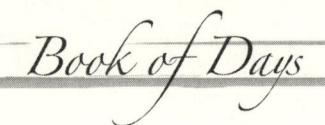

open and unencumbered. You lie in darkness and in silence. Your only company is the divine presence and the surrounding shadows. You have chosen to be here. You are unafraid.

You may even fall asleep if you are comfortable enough and inclined to do so. Give yourself plenty of time to experience this state of being. When you are ready to arise from your temple sleep, sit up, open your eyes, pick up your book of shadows, and answer the following questions.

[?] Were you able to achieve a relaxed presence of mind? How did you interpret the light within you? Were you able to visualize your aura, even as it was changing?

_____

_____

_____

[?] What images appeared to you as you closed your eyes and allowed your mind to wander? Did you receive a vision of the Goddess? How or in what form did she come to you? When in the meditation did she appear? Did you receive any messages? How do you interpret these messages?

_____

_____

_____

_____

_____

_____

Dream Interpretations

The importance of dreams can be recognized throughout the span of recorded history. In ancient Babylon, it was believed that spirits sent dreams to humankind. *The Epic of Gilgamesh* speaks of temples built to Mamu, the goddess of dreams. These sanctuaries and places of worship were expressly for those seeking protection from dreams. In Egypt, it was believed that dreams were bestowed by the gods, not by spirits, and in Memphis, many temples were erected and dedicated to Serapis, the god of dreams. The earliest known recorded dream, which belongs to King Thotmes IV, is carved upon a granite tablet that rests in between the paws of the Sphinx. Those in need of healing would visit the temple dedicated to the deity they followed and have their dreams interpreted by the priesthood there. Similarly, in ancient Greece, Aesklepius, the god of healing, would grant blessings through dreams.

Across many countries and cultures, the substance of dreams is startlingly similar. Most of us are familiar with some of the universal themes of dreams, having experienced some version of them ourselves. It is reassuring to know that no matter what part of the world you may have grown up in, the recurring messages of our psyches are not so different from one another. What makes every dreamer unique is how the universal themes unfold with regard to symbolism, locale, and interpretation.

Getting in touch with your dreams can lead you to better understanding of your emotional state during your waking hours. Self-knowledge is power, and over time you will see how this power can be translated into a beneficial aspect of your magical work.

All of our dreams are influenced by biological heritage and cultural ties; that is, our responses to and our interpretations of the world around us. Further affecting our unconscious mind is personal experience and roles in local subculture. These influences are the filters through which our dream imagery passes. They allow us to look for clues to exploring the intricate complexities that will lead to amazing discoveries.

Patricia Garfield, Ph.D. (clinical psychology), the cofounder of the Association for the Study of Dreams, has spent more than fifty years recording and compiling dreams. In an effort to link the subconscious minds of dreamers around the world, Dr. Garfield has used her many years of dream research to identify the universal dreams and their polar opposites. By interviewing numerous dreamers and by using the Internet to encourage dreamers around the world to report their experiences on her Web site, Dr. Garfield has gleaned the most common dream themes. These themes consistently transcend barriers of age, gender, culture, and geographical origin. Following, you will find these themes, how they relate to the waking world, and their possible magical implications.

DREAMS OF BEING CHASED OR ATTACKED

By far one of the most common dream motifs, the dream of being chased or attacked can often be the unconscious mind's attempt to integrate a threat you have perceived during waking hours. Pay close attention to the specific images revealed in your dream. Are you being pursued by a person, an animal, or some unknowable entity? The physical appearance of the person or thing that pursues you may provide useful clues to establishing the origin of the waking threat. Some part of you feels vulnerable, and your dream is trying to reveal this to you. Instead of giving in to the fear or terror you may experience, try to look at the imagery and symbols objectively. Keeping notes in your book of shadows may reveal the clues you need to uncover the threat so that you may take the necessary steps to protect yourself. Even a simple act, such as placing mirrors on your windowsill to reflect negative energies, may prove to be a useful charm when confronted with such a dream.

DREAMS OF BEING EMBRACED OR LOVED

Rapturous dreams bring feelings of ecstasy and desire to our dreaming minds. The feeling of being cherished and adored in a dream can be so powerful and moving that you may not wish to awaken from the comforting embrace. Many times, a dream of being loved is a manifestation of the waking desire to make a connection with a person or to connect with a special quality associated with a specific person. Look into the nature of the love that you experience in your dream. Is it a person known to you, someone with whom you already have an intimate relationship? This may be a signal from your unconscious to explore your connection to that person. The key will be found in the relationship. Perhaps you are dreaming of someone you do not personally know, for example, a celebrity or an amalgam of several people. Focus on the specific qualities the person has, and try to determine if these are qualities that you wish to invoke into your waking life. Use your grimoire to record the nature of not only who you are now, but also the person you wish to become.

DREAMS OF INJURY, ILLNESS, OR DEATH

Dreams of being injured or sick can often be so vivid that the dreamer may even experience discomfort and pain in the dream. Most often, this type of dream is a signal that you are neglecting some aspect of your waking self. When you dream of your own death, your mind is trying to tell you that an important part of yourself needs attention. Maybe there is an aspect of your life that you are not fully actualizing. If you are not actively working toward your dreams in waking life and your aspirations are lying fallow, your dream will remind you of the importance of your priorities and goals.

If you are wounded in your dream, this is a key that points to an emotional disturbance in your waking life. Emotional pain, especially anger, may reveal itself in your dreams as a physical injury. Try to look at the nature of the injury, the part of the body it is associated with, as well as any loss of function that it may cause. These will be the keys that may point you in the direction to healing the emotional pain that you are experiencing. A healing ritual will be more effective if the specific cause is known. We often build psychic walls around ourselves, and it is difficult for us to even admit when we have been hurt. Fortunately, the dreaming mind is never fooled by the exterior. Look into your heart and you will find healing.

DREAMS OF HEALING, REBIRTH, AND RENEWAL

Sometimes when we dream, all seems right with the world. We envision ourselves as complete and whole, pure of body, mind, and spirit. These dreams can be very inspiring and often relate to some type of ability we possess in our waking life that has been restored. Dreams of rebirth and healing are the dreaming mind's desire for hope for the renewal of life for a loved one or yourself. If you experience this type of dream, know that the reflection in your waking life will be one of fulfillment.

DREAMS OF CAR TROUBLE OR OTHER TRANSPORTATION TROUBLE

Sometimes in a dream, you just can't get to where you know you need to be. Your path is obstructed and forward movement is thwarted. The symbols that often manifest in these types of dreams relate to our methods of transportation. The dream images may include a car that we cannot steer or one that has lost its brakes. It may include other references to travel by trains or airplanes where an interruption or obstruction to smooth progress is evident.

These types of dreams relate to a waking scenario of diminished control. There is something in your life situation that you feel has gotten out of hand. This can relate to your level of energy, your attitude toward your environment, or your emotional state. These dreams are a clue that you may need to do more grounding and centering work in order to re-establish your relationship to yourself. You may also feel drawn to clarify boundaries in your world and better define your place within these boundaries so you can regain some of the control that you may feel has been lost.

Transportation interruptions in dreams symbolize feelings of missing out on an opportunity in life. Sometimes in your dreams, you find yourself running to catch a train only to be left behind at the station. Obstacles encountered along the way cause interference. These images and motifs translate into waking life, where there may be conditions beyond your control that hinder intentions. If your dream finds you at the train station or airport lacking your ticket or passport, this may indicate that you do not have all the information you need about the waking situation you are facing. Dreams of waiting at the train station may symbolize a transitional period in life.

Conversely, if you are able to overcome the obstacles you face in a dream, this can be interpreted as contentment and happiness with your current journey in life.

DREAMS OF PLEASURABLE TRAVEL

These dreams are often the most exhilarating. In your dreams, your ability to travel is limitless. You may find yourself racing across mountains, even flying through the air, with boundless energy. In your waking life, flying dreams or other dreams of fantastic travel directly relate to your ability to influence and affect your own destiny. These dreams portend favorable circumstances for the dreamer and will often be harbingers of satisfaction and control over your situation in waking life.

DREAMS OF LOSS OR DAMAGE TO PROPERTY

If you dream that your house has been damaged, this will likely relate to some sort of actual physical injury that you have endured in your waking life. Different parts of the house can symbolize different parts of the body: The foundation of the house symbolizes your skeleton, and the front door is a metaphor for your mouth, just as windows represent the eyes.

Recording the specific details of your dreams of property loss or damage is the key to revealing the waking injury. Likewise, a dream of losing your wallet can symbolize the loss of an aspect of your identity. A dream of losing precious jewelry relates to the loss of a valued relationship, which may be at risk. Think about what the objects in your dreams symbolize and try to relate them to things in your waking life. Often, a dream of a house infested with insects will reveal an actual physical infection that the dreamer might not be aware she has. These dreams can be a signal to heal and nourish the physical self as well as your psyche.

DREAMS OF RESTORED AND LUXURIOUS PROPERTY

Sometimes we dream of the beauty of a lush garden on the grounds of a stately mansion. Other times, we may envision our own property transformed into miraculous beauty. Maybe the images of the dream are not dramatic. They could be as simple as finding a cherished object that was once lost. Whatever the imagery, the consistent theme relates to restored physical health, new growth, and well-being in waking life. Pay attention to the object that has been restored in your dream. Dreams of ripe fruit can symbolize increased fertility. A dream of getting your wallet or purse back after it was stolen can signify a return of confidence in waking life. Thriving gardens and blooming flowers represent vitality and restored health. These dreams may be the signs that your craft is working.

DREAMS OF PERFORMING POORLY ON A TEST

No matter what phase of life we are in, many of us experience a dream of failing a test. The stress associated with being a student is often present in the subconscious mind in some form. This stress surfaces from time to time during dreams when one is facing a situation that one feels somewhat less than prepared for. These dreams can signify the fear of failure, particularly if some new waking venture is being attempted. A dream of failing a test may relate to a new or possibly unexpected challenge that you must confront in your waking life.

If you dream that you are performing before an audience in some capacity and things are not going well, this may be a signal that you are feeling unprepared to face the life challenge that lies before you. Pay special attention to the nature of the test. You will most likely find the correlation in your waking life.

DREAMS OF EXCELLENT PERFORMANCE

When you dream of a flawless performance on a test or some other kind of challenge, this is a metaphor for increased abilities in your waking life.

Enjoy this symbol of the actualization of your skills and let it reinforce your confidence. If your dream includes gaining the attention and approval of others, either through applause or some other kind of recognition, this may be a signal that you have a waking desire for greater appreciation from those around you.

DREAMS OF DROWNING OR FALLING

Falling dreams represent feelings of helplessness in waking life. Pay special attention to the location in which you are falling. The type of fall will provide insight into the waking situation that seems beyond your control. If you dream of falling from the top of a cliff, for example, this may signify that you are on the brink of danger. Falling from a very high place may mean that you have lost your support system. A fall from an amusement park ride could be a metaphor for a situation that began pleasurably, but has somehow turned threatening. It is not uncommon to awaken suddenly once you hit the ground after a dream fall. Others will sleep through this stage of the dream, and even see their bodies lying on the ground. The suddenness of hitting the ground may represent a shocking new awareness of a situation that you are facing in the waking world. Remember that dreams are reflections of the things that we hope and fear and need to confront. They are not always literal harbingers of destiny.

Dreams of drowning are also common motifs. They will often represent waking feelings of being overwhelmed. Let your dreams be your guide to revealing the aspects of your life that can benefit from positive magic. Remember to record as many details as possible. What may seem initially minor or inconsequential could possibly provide great insight into how you deal with waking situations.

DREAMS OF FLYING, SWIMMING, OR DANCING

The exhilaration of these types of dreams can be very inspiring. Contemplate the elemental correlations for the different types of dreams of utter freedom. Dreams of flying signify that you are in tune with the air element. A flying dream can also signify your connection to spirituality, or it can mean you are getting closer to achieving a cherished waking goal. A flying dream lets you know that you are free to achieve the desires of your waking mind.

Similarly, a dream of swimming confidently is a metaphor for your connection to the element of water. This may signify a balance of the emotions and the freedom to explore the hidden depths of your feelings.

Dreams of dancing joyfully correspond to the earth element. This dream is telling you that you are well grounded and ready to participate in the pleasures that life has to offer.

DREAMS OF BEING NAKED IN PUBLIC

Another common dream motif is that of appearing in public either naked, clad only in underwear, or in some other state of partial or inappropriate dress. This type of dream signifies emotional vulnerability and feelings of being exposed. You may be in a waking situation where you could be easily hurt. Perhaps you have revealed your innermost secrets to someone and are not sure if this was the right thing to do. Pay attention to how you react to your nudity in the dream. If you are trying to cover it up, you may have a weakness that you are trying to conceal in your waking life.

Sometimes we enjoy and even revel in nudity in our dreams. Rather than symbolizing vulnerability and exposure, these dreams are a metaphor for the freedom from repression or other constraints—societal, ideological, or physical. Appearing proudly naked in a dream is a sign from your dreaming mind that you possess some strong waking ability that you wish to reveal to others.

DREAMS OF BEING WELL DRESSED

Dreams of being well dressed indicate your waking confidence in your appearance or your role in life. Try to examine the clothes you are wearing in your dream to look for clues to their significance. Dreams of being dressed in wedding finery may be interpreted as the healing of a waking intimate relationship. Appearing in your dream dressed in a uniform could signify job or career success. See if the details of your dream motifs correspond with any spell work you are doing. These dreams can be affirmations that you are on the right track.

DREAMS OF TELEPHONE OR OTHER COMMUNICATION MALFUNCTIONS

If in your dream you find yourself trying to use a telephone that continuously malfunctions, this may symbolize communication difficulties in waking life. These miscommunications may not be literal at all, but may indicate some inability to express emotions that may lead to feelings of being misunderstood. Look for the symbolic and physical overtones. Are you trying to operate a phone that won't dial properly? This may be a sign that you are unsure how to connect with your partner in an intimate relationship. Are you confused over the operation of the phone or other device, such as a computer?

Perhaps you do not have enough information to fully clarify your emotional state. Light a white candle and meditate for a while before going to bed, asking the goddess to grant you clarity that you may overcome the communication difficulties you are facing.

DREAMS OF SMOOTH MECHANICAL OPERATIONS

These dreams, which are rarer than dreams of communication difficulties, may signify a new level of spiritual contact, particularly if you dream that a departed loved one has called you on the phone. This type of dream can symbolize a waking intellectual connection. You may rise in the morning with a feeling of new insight into a particular situation.

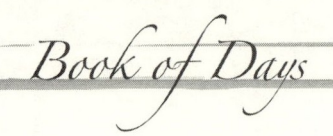

DREAMS OF NATURAL DISASTERS

Natural disasters surface in our dreams from time to time: earthquakes, hurricanes, floods, tornadoes, etc. Most often, these dreams of nature's fury point to emotional upheaval in the waking world. If you find yourself dreaming of the aftermath of a storm, this may signify emotional damage. Floods can symbolize being overwhelmed in waking life, whereas fires reflect an abundance of anger or passion. Use your connection to nature to fully explore the implications of such dreams. Do not be afraid to write down what is bothering you. Sometimes the mere act of expressing the emotions is a sufficient first step toward healing them.

DREAMS OF MIRACLES AND NATURAL BEAUTY

Sometimes, during a time of crisis, a vision of natural beauty so perfect in its form will enter into our dreams like a gift from the goddess to soothe the spirit. Dreams of flourishing gardens, crystal clear rivers, and calm waters are indicative of the reflection of our spiritual home. These dreams symbolize abundance and happiness. They represent renewal, inspiration, and the attainment of wisdom.

DREAMS OF BEING TRAPPED OR LOST

When confusion and conflict arises in waking life, it is often reflected in our dreams. We envision ourselves being trapped or lost in unfamiliar territory. Desires are elusive and we have great difficulty finding our way. If you experience such a dream, try to relate it to your waking experience. Perhaps you are faced with a choice, and the path to take is not clear. Maybe you are experiencing difficulty articulating your desires. If you cannot name that which you seek, you will not be able to call it to yourself.

Use your book of shadows to name the things you desire most, especially if they pertain to making a choice or decision that may prove difficult. Look at the specific locations in your dreams where you become lost. Try to identify clues as to the nature or source of your alienation. Seek balance in your craft and the fog will lift, revealing the true path.

DREAMS OF DISCOVERING NEW PLACES

If you find yourself making new discoveries in a dream about a familiar place, this may signify a deepening spiritual connection. Finding a new room in a house you know well may symbolize life-expanding capabilities. Since the home is also a metaphor for the body, discovering new places in a home can also indicate returning health after an illness. Dreams of opening windows may indicate increased awareness and the ability to see new possibilities. Open doors represent new beginnings and improvements in communication.

Explore these unfolding realms. They are showing you that there is more than what meets the eye. Look beyond the surface of your waking situations and interactions, and new worlds of wisdom and insight will become known to you.

DREAMS OF BEING THREATENED BY A SPIRIT

Although one of the less common universal dreams, those who experience the nightmare of being visited by an unfriendly spirit often find this dream impossible to dismiss or ignore. These dreams can be particularly frightening if the spirit is someone you knew who passed on. You may be experiencing unresolved feelings toward this person. Perhaps things were left undone or unsaid. Having a confrontational spiritual contact in your dream should not be viewed as entirely negative no matter how disturbing it may seem. It may be a part of the grieving process, particularly if the dream involves the spirit of someone who has actually died. If the spirit is not connected to an actual person, it could be a signal that a cherished part of yourself has died. Look at your dreams and goals and see if they are in alignment with your present course of action. There is a lesson for you in this dream, and you must confront your fears in order to discover its true message.

DREAMS OF BEING GUIDED BY A SPIRIT

The visitation of a spirit with a message can be a tremendously affirming dream. Sometimes a spirit who has passed beyond the veil will come back to say goodbye or let us know that all is well. Other times, a spirit will come to guide us through the difficult times in our lives, offering hope during times of grief and despair. These dreams can be tremendously comforting and may offer respite from feelings of sorrow, all while providing us with greater insight into the world beyond. Look upon these dreams for what they probably are: communication from the spiritual realm.

Recording dreams in your grimoire will enable you to become more adept at interpreting symbols. You will begin to recognize patterns of thought and emotion and ascertain how they correlate within your dream imagery. Pay attention to details and look for the magic in the mundane—therein lie the secrets of the subconscious, waiting to be revealed. You may find that your interpretations improve once you have established a consistent dream-recording ritual.

Your grimoire will be an integral part of this process of growing awareness and discovery because it will contain the records of your dreams, captured in your earliest waking moments and unspoiled by the tendency, which sets in as the day progresses, to rationalize and judge your feelings. Your grimoire is the perfect place to record the private details of your unconscious, for it is the unconscious mind we seek to bring to consciousness when we perform magic. Use your grimoire as the canvas upon which to paint an open and honest picture of your dreams, your fears, your hopes, and your aspirations. Get to know yourself all over again, and get writing.

6

Book of Lore

One of the most cherished Wiccan traditions is the Wiccan Rede, which outlines the basic tenets and rules that Wiccans live by. It is full of illustrative imagery, magical charm, ecological awareness, instruction, and plain old common sense. It is strongly recommended that the Wiccan Rede be committed to memory; it should absolutely be included in your personal book of shadows. Following is a popular version.

The Wiccan Rede

> *Bide the Wiccan Law ye must, in perfect love and perfect trust.*
> *Live and let live, fairly take and fairly give.*
> *Cast the circle thrice about, to keep all evil spirits out.*
> *To bind the spell every time, let the spell be spake in rhyme.*
> *Soft of eye and light of touch, speak ye little, listen much.*

A Witch's Grimoire

Deosil go by the waxing moon, sing and dance the witches' rune.
Widdershins go when the moon doth wane, and werewolf howls by the dread wolfsbane.
When the Lady's moon is new, kiss thy hand to her times two.
When the moon rides at her peak, then your heart's desire speak.
Heed the Northwind's mighty gale, lock the door and drop the sail.
When the wind comes from the South, love will kiss thee on the mouth.
When the wind blows from the East, expect the new and set the feast.
When the Westwind blows o'er thee, departed spirits restless be.
Nine woods in the cauldron go, burn them fast and burn them slow.
Elder be the lady's tree, burn it not or cursed be!
When the wheel begins a turn, let the Beltane fires burn.
When the wheel hath turned to Yule, light the log and let Pan rule.
Heed ye flower, bush and tree, and by the Lady, blessed be!
Where the rippling waters flow, cast a stone and truth you'll know.
Whenever ye have a need, harken not to other's greed.
With the fool no season spend, nor be counted as his friend.
Merry meet and merry part, bright the cheeks and warm the heart.
Mind the threefold law ye should, three times bad and three times good.
When misfortune is enow, wear the blue star on your brow.
True in love ever be, unless thy love is false to thee.
Eight words the Wiccan Rede fulfill: "An' it harm none, do what ye will!"

Copy the Rede directly into your book of shadows. Because the Rede explicates the tenets of magical practice, instructions for casting the circle, and essential references to the Sabbats, no true Wiccan grimoire can be considered complete without it.

The Charge of the Goddess

Nearly every witch has experienced the desire to draw the energy of the Goddess into her- or himself. For the veteran priestess and priest, this is often done as a part of ritual known as "drawing down the moon." The priestess and priest work in tandem, with the priest invoking the great Goddess and the priestess receiving the energy of the Goddess into herself. The priestess then radiates this power outward through the circle. This practice is not exclusive to female/male working relationships. It is possible to attain divine consciousness on one's own, as communion with the deities is bestowed directly by the Goddess and not by any other person. Still, it is important to learn the origin of this sacred invocation, as it is widely used in many different traditions.

In 1890, Charles G. Leland published his accounts of various interviews he conducted with an Italian *strega* (sorceress or witch) in whose original handwriting the earliest known version of the Charge of the Goddess was given, and whose true identity remains unknown. It is believed that the practices of her specific craft existed as an oral tradition, many of which have survived to this day. The focus of the *strega's* particular tradition of Italian witchcraft is on the Roman goddess Diana, who gives birth to a daughter, Aradia.

This is perhaps the earliest tradition of Dianic witchcraft, which is now primarily associated with exclusively female covens. In the past, Dianic witchcraft was more closely associated with the worship of the divine moon goddess, personified by Diana and Aradia, than with a strictly feminine agenda. In this passage, Diana has instructed Aradia how to craft spells and ward off enemies, and now Aradia imparts her knowledge to others:

A Witch's Grimoire

When I shall have departed from this world,
Whenever ye have need of anything,
Once in the month, and when the moon is full,
Ye shall assemble in some desert place,
Or in a forest all together join
To adore the potent spirit of your queen,
My mother, great Diana. She who fain
Would learn all sorcery yet has not won
Its deepest secrets, then my mother will
Teach her, in truth all things as yet unknown.
And ye shall be free from all slavery,
And so shall ye be free in everything;
And as the sign that ye are truly free,
Ye shall be naked in your rites, both men
And women also: this shall last until
The last of your oppressors shall be dead;
And ye shall make the game of Benevento,
Extinguishing the lights, and after that
Shall hold your supper thus.

What follows in *Aradia, Gospel of the Witches* are the instructions for consecrating the meal, conjuring sacred cakes with wine, salt, and honey and then forming them into a crescent shape before baking. Consider the age of this verse, and compare it to the more modern versions of the Charge of the Goddess found in other books. You will be able to determine the evolution of the modern charge from its origins in the Aradia gospel. This evolution is an excellent example of the techniques you should be developing as you use this book: how to take the wisdom that has been handed down and make it truly your own.

Book of Lore

The Song of Amergin

The Song of Amergin is one of the earliest examples of Celtic poetic mythology. Dating back to circa 1268 B.C.E., the song is an Irish liturgical hymn and could very well be used as an oracle or the charge of the god. Consisting of metaphoric statements interspersed with queries, the Song of Amergin has been interpreted by Robert Graves to have direct correlations with the ancient Celtic calendar and alphabet. In Graves' translation, the Song of Amergin is a journey through the wheel of the year told through the beautiful poetic imagery of a Druidic bard:

> *I am a stag: of seven tines,*
> *I am a flood across a plain,*
> *I am a wind on a deep lake,*
> *I am a tear the Sun lets fall,*
> *I am a hawk above the cliff,*
> *I am a thorn beneath the nail,*
> *I am a wonder among flowers,*
> *I am a wizard: who but I*
> *Sets the cool head aflame with smoke?*
> *I am a spear that roars for blood,*
> *I am a salmon in a pool,*
> *I am a lure from paradise,*
> *I am a hill where poets walk,*
> *I am a boar ruthless and red,*
> *I am a breaker threatening doom,*
> *I am a tide that drags to death,*
> *I am an infant: who but I*
> *Peeps from the unhewn dolmen arch?*
> *I am the womb of every holt,*
> *I am the blaze on every hill,*

A Witch's Grimoire

I am the queen of every hire,
I am the shield for every head,
I am the tomb of every hope.

Consider the rich images contained in this verse. Does it not imply that the spirits of nature are irrevocably connected to the spirit of the gods and goddesses?

Learn to see that divine grace can be discovered anywhere—in hopes and fears, in achievements and disappointments, in shadow and light, in joy and pain, in life and death. All are valid expressions of divine consciousness. Use your own personal experiences to enhance your writing. Think about the mundane ways in which you experience the deities on a subtle level and how the Goddess and God inhabit those attributes.

[?] Make a list of all the different places in the world where you see the proof of divine immanence and use this list as a framework to write an original invocation celebrating the aspect of goddess and god closest to your heart. Travel through the space of a year in your mind and think about the changing face of the divine.

_____

_____

_____

_____

Book of Lore

The Great Wheel

In the first chapter, we explored some ancient origins of the modern worship of the divine feminine. Across many lands and many centuries, the myths of old speak of a goddess who brings life to earth. This goddess then descends into the underworld and loses everything—her power, her identity, her true love, or all of the above. Through recognition of her powerful divine essence, her supremacy is restored, and life on earth once again flourishes.

When we consider how ancient people were utterly dependent on the fruits of the earth for their survival in such an immediate way, these stories take on much greater significance. The survival of the people was irrevocably and directly linked to the survival of the crops, the success of the hunt, and the forces of nature. It is no small wonder that the worship of the Goddess prevailed, for it was only by her favor that life would be ensured to continue.

Another telling of this tale involves the relationship between the mother Goddess and her consort. In the cold of winter on the shortest day, the return of the light is welcomed and the god is considered to be reborn. We travel with the Goddess and her son or consort to the first light in the dark of winter, the time of awakening and initiation. The seasons change, spring arrives, and the earth begins to thrive, sending forth tangible evidence of the new life that abounds. As time progresses, the Goddess and her son or consort are joined in the sacred union of fertility, and the full heat of summer brings the earth to its fullest bounty. Summer days begin to fade and so does the power of the god. He is harvested, cut down like the fields of wheat, only to rise again. Other descriptions of this myth involve two separate aspects of the god: the Oak King and the Holly King. They are both rivals and lovers to the Goddess, and each has his season. As the year waxes, the Oak King reigns until his twin, the Holly King, overthrows him. The Holly King presides over the waning year until his death, after which he is reborn as the Oak King.

Whether your tradition focuses on the descent and resurrection of only the Goddess, the relationship between the Goddess and the God, or the

A Witch's Grimoire

rivalry for the Goddess between her two consorts, this cycle of birth, growth, consummation, death, and rebirth is celebrated in the Wheel of the Year in much the same way.

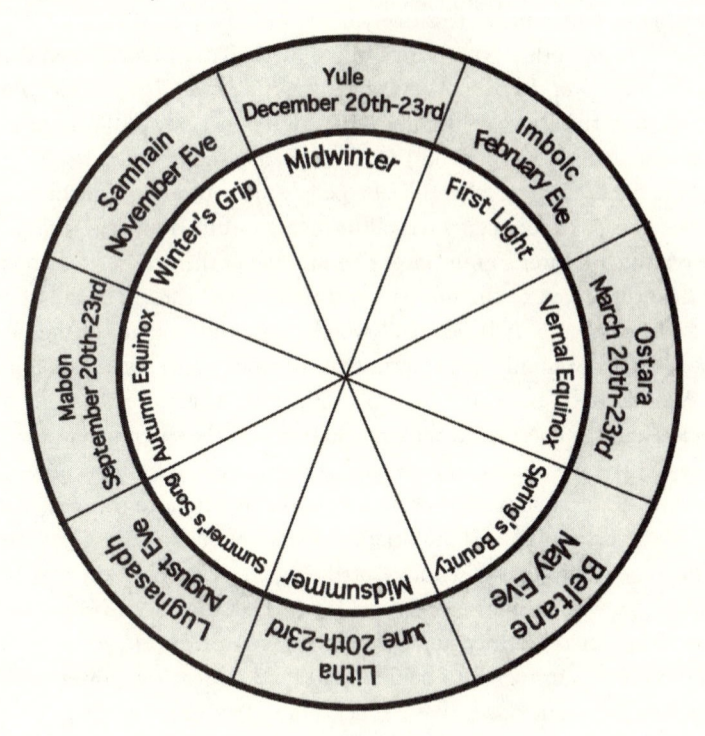

Wheel of the Year diagram:
- Yule — December 20th-23rd — Midwinter
- Imbolc — February Eve — First Light
- Ostara — March 20th-23rd — Vernal Equinox
- Beltane — May Eve — Spring's Bounty
- Litha — June 20th-23rd — Midsummer
- Lugnasadh — August Eve — Summer's Song
- Mabon — September 20th-23rd — Autumn Equinox
- Samhain — November Eve — Winter's Grip

The Sabbats

The witches' sabbats are seasonal festivals that mark the changing of the four seasons, the turning of the Great Wheel, also called the Wheel of the Year. Evidence of the cultural importance of these sabbats can be found in the relics of the Celts and other ancient people of Great Britain and Ireland, who built impressive monuments—with architectural precision far beyond what people of that era were thought to possess—to mark the solstices and equinoxes. Ancient stone circles attest to the fact that the solstices were acknowledged and revered with great significance by early peoples. Just outside of Amesbury, England, is Stonehenge, perhaps the most famous stone circle of all. While the true meaning of its intended function is unknown and its spiritual implications are subject to speculation, one thing is for certain: Every year, like clockwork, on the summer solstice, a ray of light travels into the center of the circle, illuminating the central altar stone and surrounding stones with undeniable precision. To this day, modern neo-Druids make the pilgrimage to Stonehenge to celebrate with reverence the longest day of the year, regardless of whether they are permitted within the actual circle, as they once were, or not.

In Ireland, hollow hills were constructed out of stones stacked so carefully they have remained watertight and in place for thousands of years. Inside each mound is a pathway that leads to a chamber. The most famous of these mysterious monuments are the hollow hills of Newgrange and Knowth. At Newgrange on the winter solstice, a sunbeam will travel down a narrow corridor, illuminating the interior chamber for approximately seventeen minutes at dawn. A similar phenomenon occurs at Knowth on the autumn equinox.

These impressive monuments took several generations to build, and the stones used to erect them were carried over great distances made even more vast by the limitations of the times in which they were built. Those who began the construction did not live to see it completed, nor did their children. It wasn't until a later generation of builders that the final monuments were completed.

Imagine the great importance that these places of pilgrimage and worship had to the people who conceived of them. The builders knew they would never see the monuments' completion, yet somehow they were able to inspire future generations to preserve the planetary reverence that would survive for thousands of years. All this work was done to create what, in essence, is a calendar undeniably used to mark the turning points that modern Wiccans now celebrate as the sabbats.

YULE, THE WINTER SOLSTICE

The first sabbat of the year, Yule, is celebrated on the day of winter solstice, which usually occurs between December 20 and December 23. The winter solstice is the shortest day of the year, the time when the earth is farthest away from the sun in her orbit through space. Yule is hailed as the return of the light because the winter solstice is the turning point at which the days begin to lengthen again. In ritual, this natural occurrence is the allegory of the rebirth of the god. The infant Sun King is born and the return of the light is celebrated. On this festival of the longest night, rituals invoking star goddesses are common, the Yule log is adorned with holly, and candles are lit to hail the coming lengthening of days. A beautiful Yule ritual is to craft and consecrate the Yule log, set it with festive candles, and light each candle as a different goddess is invoked. Yule is the sabbat of rebirth.

OSTARA, THE SPRING EQUINOX

The festival of Ostara is the first day of spring, usually occurring between March 20 and March 23. It is a turning point on the wheel as day and night are in equal balance. Sometimes it is known as the Day of the Phoenix, a name that acknowledges the theme of rebirth, as the phoenix rises from its own ashes to take flight once again. The equilibrium of light and darkness, male and female, and the return of abundant flora to the earth are celebrated through ritual. Ostara is the sabbat of new beginnings. In Christian tradition the resurrection of Christ also signifies a new beginning, which is appropriate for the time of year.

LITHA, THE SUMMER SOLSTICE

Litha marks the longest day of the year and is celebrated on the summer solstice, which usually falls between June 20 and June 23. At this time, the earth is at her fullest bounty and abundance. Trees are lush with leaves, and the spring flowers give way to summer fruits. The sun is at its brightest, and the Goddess and the God are celebrated in the full glory of life and nature. On the longest day, the radiance of light is celebrated, as are the plentiful gifts of the earth. Summer is at its peak, the faeries frolic, and it seems as though the days will never end. We bask in the light during this time of fruition and realization. Litha is the sabbat of culmination.

MABON, THE AUTUMNAL EQUINOX

On Mabon, the autumnal equinox, we once again reflect on themes of balance and harmony. This is the time to build the bridge between the worlds of the masculine and feminine so that we may walk freely between them with respect and understanding. Equal day and equal night brings us to the realization that the days are growing shorter and that the time for harvest is near. Mabon is the time when we reap the benefits of the work we have done throughout the year. Since very few of us live under the direct influence of an agricultural society anymore, it is useful to think of the harvest in metaphorical terms. What new beginnings did you celebrate early in spring? How close did you come to achieving your goals? Mabon is the sabbat of balance. On Mabon, set your altar with the cornucopia and reflect on the gifts bestowed upon you by the Goddess. Her bounty is your fulfillment. When you bring the harvest into the home, your life is filled with abundance and peace.

A Witch's Grimoire

Cross-Quarter Days

Between the sabbats are cross-quarter days of celebration that herald the passing of time and the gradual turn of the seasons. Although we celebrate sabbats on the solstices and equinoxes (at the exact planetary moments of true transition where one season ends and another begins), in life it seems as though the seasons change slowly and gradually, blending into one another. The cross-quarter days enable us to prepare for and celebrate the more subtle changes of the new aspects of the dawning season.

IMBOLC, SPRING'S APPROACH

Imbolc, or Candlemas, celebrated between the eve of February and the second of February, is when we experience the first return of the light. It is the cross-quarter day between the winter solstice and the spring equinox. Imbolc is traditionally the time for initiations, new beginnings, and rebirth. If you have already been initiated, Imbolc is a perfect time to rededicate yourself anew to your chosen path. If you are a neophyte, Imbolc is the time to make the passage into the inner circles. Sacred to the goddess Brigid, whose attributes are poetry, healing, and smithcraft, Imbolc celebrations may include festive candle-lighting and the creation of a Brigid's cross, a four-way equal-arm cross motif made from folded straw. The priestess may even wear a crown of candles. In the secular world, Imbolc corresponds with Groundhog Day, when secular folks turn to one of nature's creatures to get a glimpse of the timing of spring.

BELTANE, SPRING'S BOUNTY

As the sacred Beltane fires burn, it is the time to celebrate joy and sexuality. Beltane is also known as May Day and is usually celebrated on May 1. Just as in days of old, modern witches adorn and dance around the Maypole with its many colored ribbons and highly symbolic theme of sexual union between the Goddess and the God. In the more innocent version of

Book of Lore

the Maypole, the rites of spring are celebrated as general fertility and prayers for abundance rather than just sexual desire and fulfillment. Beltane is one point on the Wheel of the Year at which the veil between the worlds grows thin. It is said that on Beltane it is possible to commune with the faery folk, who are nearer now to us than they will be for months. Faery lore claims that on Beltane, the faery kingdom holds court inside a hollow hill that may vanish at any time and magically reappear on the other side of the world. This is part of the reason why great caution must be exercised when coming into contact with the faeries. No one knows if you will be enraptured for just moments or for a lifetime.

LUGNASADH, SUMMER'S SONG

Lugnasadh, or Lammastide, is usually celebrated on August Eve or August 1. The cross-quarter day in between the summer solstice and the autumnal equinox, Lugnasadh is a magical time when the god of summer begins to lay down his crown and give up his reign as the time for harvest draws near. Like the summer grass, he is cut down with the knowledge that he will be reborn again. On Lugnasadh, we stand suspended in time, between hope and fear. Much of our work for the year is done, but the final results have not yet manifested. The crops are cut and lying in the fields, but they have not yet been brought into the home as the harvest. Lammas is traditionally the time for handfasting, when lovers commit to a mutually exclusive relationship for a year and a day. Their hands are joined and tied with a ribbon. If after a year and a day has passed, and they still wish to remain in each others' company, the handfasting can be renewed for another year and a day, or the couple can jump the broom in a symbolic union of the souls. Many modern weddings include the phrase "until death do us part," but in the witches' wedding, the souls are thought to be joined both in this life and in the next. If, after a year and a day, the couple finds that they no longer desire each other's company, a handparting is done and the exclusive relationship is thought to have run its course.

SAMHAIN, WINTER'S GRIP

Samhain is the final turn of the wheel before the year begins again. Celebrated as the witch's New Year, Samhain is the other point on the wheel at which the veil between the worlds grows thin. Celebrated on October 31, Samhain is a solemn ritual wherein the witch acknowledges those who have passed on to the spirit world. Stories are told, names are called, libations are poured, and the spirits are invited to take part in the ritual. Beloveds are remembered, ancestors are honored, and the spirit world is thought to coexist with the earthly plane more closely than usual. When one calls upon the departed spirit of a loved one on Samhain night, it is not at all unusual for the departed person to show up and make his or her presence known in some way. In our modern society, Samhain is celebrated as Halloween, when encounters with witches are common and carved pumpkins glow to light the way for benevolent spirits and to frighten away the undesirable. In the Christian church, the day after Samhain, November 1, is celebrated as All Saints' Day, and November 2 is All Souls' Day, both days honoring those who have departed the earthly realm.

Esbats

The esbats are days that the coven gathers, or the solitary witch enacts rituals of her own that do not fall on one of the sabbats or cross-quarter days. Generally, esbat rituals are not as elaborate as those planned for a sabbat, yet they give continuity and meaning to the practice of Wicca and enhance the work at hand. Whether you belong to a coven or practice solitary, you will still experience the community and fellowship of like-minded people because you can be certain that on a full moon night, circles are being cast across the world. Picture yourself as an integral part of this global community. By realizing your connection to all, you will also bring yourself closer to your connection to the divine.

Book of Lore

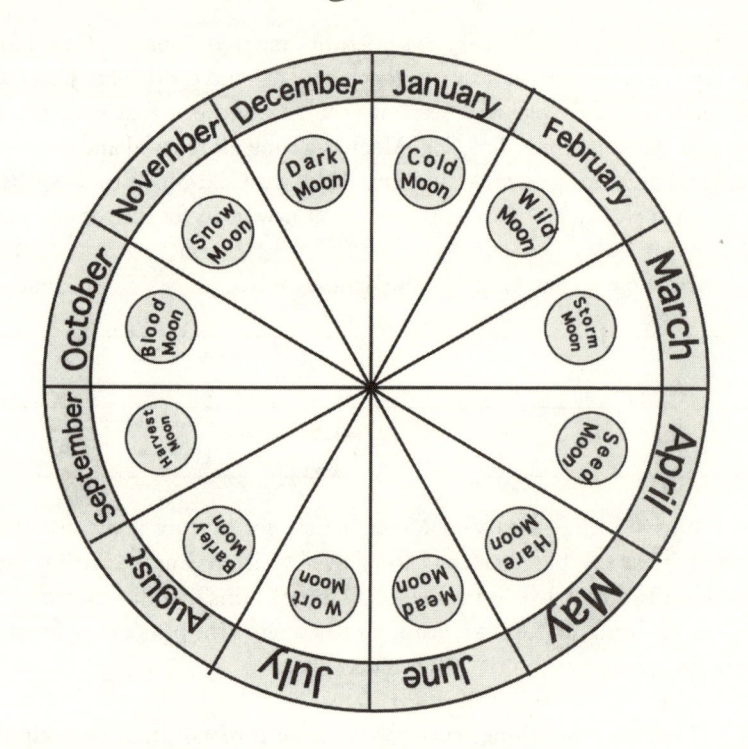

FULL MOON

Most esbats are celebrated on the full moon and/or the new moon. On the full moon, the radiance of the Goddess shines in the night sky. Even the brightness of the stars appears lessened by her brilliance. Her shining body hangs like a voluptuous pearl against the surrounding darkness. The full moon calls witches to gather and honor her divine power.

Every full moon has a different aspect as we travel through the year. Use the specific characteristics of each full moon to guide you as you create your rituals.

A Witch's Grimoire

The full moon in January is sometimes referred to as the Cold Moon. January is named for the Roman god Janus. Mythology depicts Janus as a god with two faces, one that sees into the past and one that sees into the future at the same time. The Cold Moon is a time for renewal and for discovering and dedicating purpose and focus. Use the Cold Moon to do spells to bring about wealth and prosperity, and to set new goals for the coming year.

[?] Write down a few ideas for your January esbat.

_____

_____

_____

February brings the Wild Moon, a time for healing and purification. February's name is based on the Latin *februa*, which means "to purify." Since Imbolc, or February Eve, is the defining sabbat of this month, any spells that prepare for initiation, invoke healing or new growth, physical or financial, would be appropriate on the Wild Moon.

[?] Think on those things that you most need to call unto yourself, and write down your thoughts for the February esbat.

_____

_____

_____

March is named for Mars, the Roman god of war. March brings us the Storm Moon and the time for the manifestation of the goals set under the Cold Moon. The snow melts and life begins to grow and prosper once again.

Book of Lore

Think of spells for personal growth to enact on the Storm Moon. Perhaps there is an aspect of yourself or a certain behavior you would really like to change. Although change is difficult, it is a necessary part of the transformative process. Without change, stagnation occurs and progression remains unattainable.

{ ? } Write down something you would most like to achieve, or something about yourself or your environment you would benefit by changing.

_____

_____

_____

The month of April is dedicated to Aphrodite, the Greek goddess of love. As her name is seemingly rooted in *aperire,* meaning "to open," the full moon aspect of April is the Seed Moon. Spells for love are appropriate at this time, as are spells for balance, cleansing, and strengthening.

{ ? } Meditate on the things in life you really love, or the love that you one day hope to attain. Surround yourself with loving thoughts and write down ideas for your April esbat.

_____

_____

_____

May is the time when the spring flowers burst forth and the fertility of the earth is evident in the flora and fauna of the blessed land. The full moon aspect of May is the Hare Moon, regarded so for the amazing reproductive abilities of this woodland creature. May is also the sacred month of Mary, the Virgin Mother of God. With these thoughts in mind, develop a Hare Moon ritual that celebrates either the joy and pleasure of sexuality or the peace and centeredness of abstinence; whichever will most benefit your work. If you have endured sexual violence or trauma in your past, the Hare Moon would be a good time to enact rituals designed to heal this part of yourself. Embrace yourself as a sacred sexual being, whether that means enjoying your sexuality or reserving it through celibacy. Remember that part of the beauty of sexuality is union.

[?] Meditate on things you would like to bring into being through themes of cooperation, togetherness, and understanding. Write down ideas for a Hare Moon esbat.

_____

_____

_____

June brings us the Mead Moon, or Honey Moon. Dedicated to the Roman Goddess Juno, wife of Jupiter, king of the gods, the month of June is associated with marriage. This is the origin of the customary June brides and why June is such a popular month for weddings to this day. The tradition of the honeymoon comes from the custom of the bride and groom drinking wine made from honey, which is also known as mead, each day for one month following their nuptials. Ideas for rituals for the Mead Moon include strengthening bonds between friends or beloveds, spells to improve communication, and rites to acknowledge the turning point of solstice, the lengthening and shortening of days.

Book of Lore

[?] Think of these concepts of strengthening bonds and partnerships as you develop your ideas for the Mead Moon esbat.

The full moon aspect of July is the Wort Moon. "Wort" is another term for "herb," and the Wort Moon hails the coming harvest as we observe the very first signs of agricultural maturation. The fields grow ripe with what is soon to be the harvest. In July, we first notice the days growing shorter and we prepare to reap the benefits of our hard work. Spells for protection and prosperity are appropriate for this full moon. There may be many hopes and dreams that you wish to manifest during the harvest time. Perhaps there is still preparation to be done.

[?] Create a brief magical "to do" list to guide you in crafting your July esbat.

August's full moon aspect is the Barley Moon. The Barley Moon is a time for gathering together, whether "gathering" suggests the crops in the field or the gathering of companions to the circle. On the Barley Moon, reflect upon your connection to all people and things; recognize your similarity to all beings. Appreciate your individuality while enjoying the things you have in common with others. Prepare a magical feast to share, especially one that contains bread or grain. When we refer to something as "august"

A Witch's Grimoire

(as an adjective), we compliment the person or event as dignified, majestic, and grand.

[?] Concentrate on the higher aspects of human nature and attempt spells that will enhance your wisdom. Bring people together to share thoughts, ideas, and goals. Let your companions inspire you as you create a Barley Moon esbat.

_____

_____

_____

The theme of harvest surfaces in earnest during September. In July and August, preparations for the harvest are made; the full moon of September is the time for the realization of creative projects that began earlier in the year, the fruition of magical intentions, and completion of circles. Also called the Harvest Moon, the September full moon is the time for giving thanks for goals realized, projects completed, and wisdom gained. Make an offering to the Goddess to show your appreciation for her presence in her life.

[?] Reflect on the positive changes you have experienced, and the right expression will become known to you. Focus on activities that will help bring things into balance. Write down things you are thankful for to form the basis of your Harvest Moon esbat.

_____

_____

_____

Book of Lore

October brings the Blood Moon. The full moon aspect of October is full of memory, making it an auspicious time for releasing old patterns and energies, remembering those who have passed on, and clearing away psychic debris. Winter's approach is felt at this time, and spells to address imbalances or which focus on the reversal of ill luck are good choices. October's full moon is sacred to the Goddess in her crone aspect. Meditate on her wisdom and her promise of rebirth. Think about how far you have come, and yet how far you still have to go.

{ ? } Write down a short list of things you need to let go of in order to progress and make room for the new. Create a ritual around releasing these entities for your Blood Moon esbat.

_____

_____

_____

November's full moon aspect is the Snow Moon. The chill of the cold is in the air and the nights grow long. The Snow Moon rituals should be focused on divination and receiving guidance. Close to the time when the veil between the worlds is thin, it is still possible to communicate with the spirits. Remember the names and stories of those who have departed and ask for their aid. Prepare for the long darkness that lies ahead by lighting candles and gazing into your crystals for enlightenment and answers. Open your mind to receiving prophecies of things to come.

A Witch's Grimoire

{ ? } Write down your vision of the future as the first step toward actualizing it. Let these ideas become the basis for the Snow Moon esbat.

_____

_____

_____

As the days are at their shortest and the nights their longest, December's gift to us is the Dark Moon. December's full moon aspect manifests in the need for introspection, silence, and stillness. So often as children, we are taught to fear the dark. Now is the time for releasing the mind from useless apprehension and facing the darkness with honor and respect. It is in the darkness of the mother's womb that new life is created. Out of the darkness of the night sky are the stars revealed in contrast. In the dark corners of the mind are the fantasies of dreams revealed. Take the time to meditate in silence on darkness. Allow yourself to be at peace with the winter stillness. Do not feel obligated to fill the void with idle chatter. Let yourself be as silent as a snowflake. Reflect on the mysteries of darkness.

{ ? } Write down a fear that you have that you would like to banish. Approach your work with calmness and reverence as you write down some ideas for your December esbat.

_____

_____

_____

NEW MOON

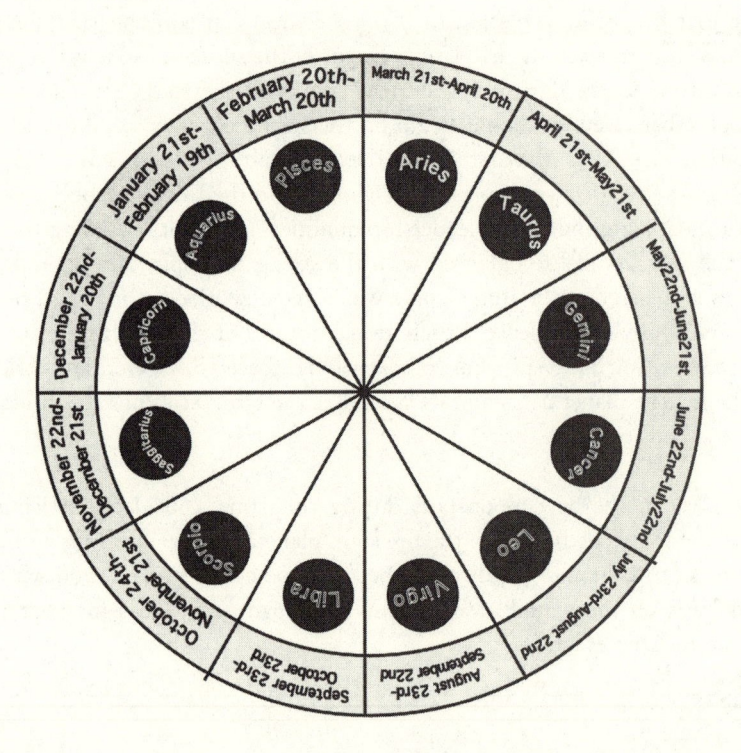

Just as the full moon nights shine forth the beauty of the Goddess, so too does the more subtle energy of the new moon glorify her presence in a different but no less significant way. In the absence of the light of the moon, the stars shine with more intensity and we are able to behold the complexity of the constellations, to see and experience the stars and planets. The moon turns her dark side to us, enabling us to contemplate the mysteries of the unseen. For these reasons, the new moon esbats are ideally suited for divinations, the consulting of oracles, and planetary magic.

A Witch's Grimoire

You can create effective new moon esbats that will carry you throughout the year by paying attention to the astrological constellation that the sun passes through each month. Use the signs of the zodiac as your guide when you attune to the dark night and the beauty of the starry sky. Your new moon esbat calendar should begin on the spring equinox, marking its correlation with Aries, the first sign of the zodiac after the equinox.

Aries is a fire sign, representing vitality and the life force. Because it is a cardinal sign, indicating leadership qualities, group rituals using themes of the newness of life balanced with the strength of spirit are appropriate. Aries is the sign of the infant soul. When the new moon is in Aries, reflect on your individual essence. Recall awakenings from childhood, perhaps the time when you had a spiritual epiphany and discovered the Goddess. Aries is ruled by the planet Mars and its symbol is the ram. Aries begins on March 21 and ends on April 20.

{ ? } When the new moon falls during this time, consider practicing elemental magic dedicated to the fire sign, planetary magic dealing with the aspects of Mars, and rituals concerned with objectivity and action with an emphasis on individual awareness. Write down some ideas for your new moon in Aries esbat.

The new moon in Taurus is an esbat for blossoming. Taurus is a fixed earth sign, meaning its characteristics are organization and groundedness. Ruled by the planet Venus and symbolized by the bull, Taurus is the sign of innocence and youth whose attributes include focus, concentration, and the creation of sacred space. Taurus begins on April 21 and continues through May 21.

Book of Lore

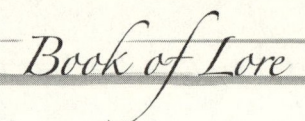

[?] When the new moon falls during this time, your esbat should include rededicating your altar, elemental magic dealing with the aspects of earth, or explorations of the associations with the planet Venus, most notably its associations with the goddess of love. Write down some ideas for your esbat for a new moon in Taurus.

_____

_____

_____

    The next zodiacal phase brings us into the realm of Gemini, the twins. Gemini is the mutable air sign whose aspects deal with communication. Mercury, the messenger of the gods, rules Gemini. Gemini represents the adolescent soul, and its span runs from May 22 to June 21, on or around the sabbat of Litha. The air is the most intangible of the elements and Gemini is a mutable sign, so rituals dealing with communicating with spirits would be an appropriate. Focus on the spiritual aspects of air, and the sending and receiving of messages. Remember that if Mercury is in its retrograde phase of orbit, communication in general will prove to be difficult. Light a blue candle and meditate on the throat chakra to overcome any obstacles that are interfering with your ability to communicate.

[?] Contemplate the duality of the Gemini twins as reflected in the duality of nature: male and female, body and spirit. Look upon the first magnitude stars of Castor and Pollux that make up the constellation. Think also on the attributes of adolescence with its sense of freedom, fearlessness, and discovery as you craft your new moon in Gemini esbat. Write down some of your ideas here.

A Witch's Grimoire

The sign of Cancer brings us into the age of the bride and bridegroom. From June 22 until July 22, the cardinal water sign of the crab influences our life. Ruled by the moon, Cancer represents the mother aspect. Think of how the moon affects the tides to understand the new moon energies of Cancer. As the mother is the source of knowledge, wisdom, and inspiration, the nurturing instinct flows from her to us. Likewise, the river flows to the sea just as moonlight travels through the sky to meet us.

[?] Plan a new moon ritual that deals with elemental water: water as the source of life like the mother, water as the seat of the emotions, water as a metaphor for intuition. Think of Cancer's cardinal quality as a call to action. Use your imagination and sensitivity to craft a new moon esbat. Write some ideas here.

Like the sun that shines brightly upon the earth, Leo is the fixed fire sign that embodies the father aspect. Representing the age of maturity, Leo's traits of vitality, nobility, and strength correspond with the waning summer from July 23 to August 22. Symbolized by the lion, Leo's characteristics also include warmth and generosity as well as sexuality and self-expression. Solar energy dominates the sign of Leo, and rituals that celebrate the sun gods or goddesses are appropriate themes for a new moon esbat, as are rituals that deal with elemental fire.

Book of Lore

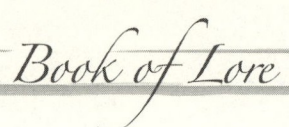

[?] Carve and dedicate a candle to a sacred purpose or your heart's desire. Let the glowing flame upon your altar be your guide through the lengthening night. Keep the radiant energy of the sun close to your heart, even as you celebrate on a dark moon night. Use your creativity to write ideas for a new moon in Leo esbat.

_____

_____

_____

The dichotomy of stability and constancy coexisting with change and versatility is the essence of the mutable earth sign, Virgo. Ruled by Mercury, Virgo is symbolized by the virgin, whose attributes include clarity and discrimination. Virgo begins on August 23 and continues until September 22. This corresponds to the autumnal equinox and the commencement of the harvest season, marking Virgo's association with advancing maturity. Meditate on dreams that have been realized, accomplishments that have been achieved, and times when you have used your unique intuition for discernment to inspire your new moon esbat.

[?] Since Virgo's symbol is the virgin, plan a ritual to honor the maiden aspect of the Goddess. Think of Persephone, who descends to the underworld at the time of the equinox to bring about the change of the seasons. Think of aspects of your life you would like to change and incorporate these ideas to give your new moon esbat a significant purpose. Write down your ideas here.

_____

_____

_____

A Witch's Grimoire

The scales of balance are the symbol of Libra, which begins on September 23, just after the autumnal equinox, and continues until October 23. It is no coincidence that the balancing aspects of Libra coincide with the equality of day and night. It is the quest for balance, more so than the achievement of balance, that gives Libra a complex nature. As the cardinal air sign, Libra is represented by spiritual light and by the attributes of gentleness, intelligence, justice, and charm. Ruled by Venus, the morning and evening star, Libra's rituals should involve healing and balancing relationships. The age of Libra is the age of achievement, the time in which the fruits of the harvest manifest in life. Your new moon in Libra esbat may include love spells, a wand meditation and consecration, or rituals that seek to assist the attainment of emotional balance.

[?] Think of the gifts of Venus, the goddess of love, or the Egyptian goddess Ma'at who holds the scales of judgment. Weigh your heart against her mythical feather as you prepare for your new moon in Libra esbat. Write down a few of your ideas here.

_____

_____

_____

The dominion of Scorpio begins on October 24 and continues until November 21. Symbolized by the scorpion, this mutable fire sign represents the age of introspection. Ruled by Pluto, the attributes of Scorpio are self-control, willpower, magnetism, and insight. When a mystery is revealed, the revelation may often feel like the scorpion's sting. Scorpio deals with the unseen aspects of nature, for example the deep roots of the tree. The roots are evident by the fact that the tree thrives. Because they are hidden beneath

Book of Lore

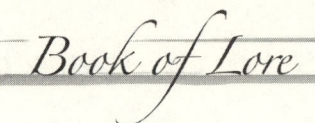

the ground, however, we know of their existence more through the manifestation of results rather than direct observation. Use the attributes of Scorpio to guide you in crafting a new moon esbat during this time. Meditation and introspection are necessary here, as is magic dealing with the unseen energies of nature that we nonetheless know to be evident.

[?] Contemplate the mysteries of Pluto, king of the dark underworld, and write some ideas for your new moon in Scorpio esbat.

_____

_____

_____

Sagittarius brings us the mutable fire sign symbolized by the centaur. From November 22 until December 21, the half-man, half-horse shoots his arrows of inspiration into our lives. Ruled by the planet Jupiter, the attributes of Sagittarius are honesty, daring, and enthusiasm. Use this time to project your desires into your ability to effect change in your life. After all, this is the core concept of spell crafting. Sagittarius represents the age of honor. Power and influence are felt most strongly during this time. Think of the arrows of Sagittarius as bolts of lightning. Inspiration comes suddenly, brilliantly, and is gone in an instant. Be at the ready for illumination to strike at any moment. Meditate on goddesses of supreme power, such as Hera or Juno. As the reign of Sagittarius draws to a close, the light of Yule returns to us.

[?] Think of areas in your life in which you need inspiration, and write some ideas for your new moon in Sagittarius esbat here.

A Witch's Grimoire

The sign of Capricorn ushers in the age of wisdom. Ruled by Saturn, the cardinal earth sign of Capricorn runs from December 22 to January 20. Symbolized by the mythical sea-goat, Capricorn can be interpreted as the balance between primordial instinct (symbolized by the sea) and natural law (symbolized by the mountain). These two aspects of nature give Capricorn its unique qualities of stability, tranquility, and wisdom. Capricorn is the time for pulling back and observing the effects of the work you have done this year. Rituals and spells for this time should reflect bringing magic into your daily life. Think of areas in your life that are mundane that you would like to make sacred. This could mean an aspect of your career that you wish to dedicate to the goddess. A simple household chore can take on greater significance when viewed through the lens of divine awareness. Dusting a table becomes consecrating an altar. Baking bread becomes preparing a magical feast. Organizing your closet becomes clearing away stagnant energies and discarding old ways.

[?] Think of ways to incorporate divine blessing into your daily life. Write down your ideas for your new moon in Capricorn esbat here.

Book of Lore

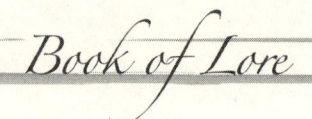

The new moon in Aquarius brings us themes of rebirth and immortality. Symbolized by the water bearer, Aquarius is a fixed air sign ruled by the planet Uranus from January 21 until February 19. During Aquarius, focus on the gifts of the water bearer combined with the energies of air. A ritual dedicated to the goddess Iris, who skates down the rainbow, would be appropriate for this time. Chakra-balancing rituals would also have an affinity with Aquarius, as the chakras are perceived as containing all the colors of the rainbow. The attributes of Aquarius are vision, tolerance, originality, and individuality. The age of Aquarius corresponds with the age of the crone, the time for recognizing wisdom gained and imparting it to others.

[?] Think of the magical practices you would most like to share with others, spells that have worked, charms that have empowered you. Write down your ideas for a new moon in Aquarius esbat.

_____

_____

_____

With Pisces comes the age of death, the point on the zodiac at which the soul is believed to have incarnated previously through all other signs and is now ready to leave the cycle of birth, death, and rebirth. Pisces brings with it a culmination of spiritual awareness. As a mutable water sign ruled by Neptune, the gifts of Pisces are transformation and love. Pisces begins on February 20 and lasts until March 20, just before the day of the Phoenix, the soul's renewal on the vernal equinox. Pisces exists in a dreamlike state. Its attributes are compassion, comprehension, humility, and psychic awareness. Meditate on the three-pronged symbol of the trident for insight into Pisces' dreamy, watery realm. Call upon the Nine Muses to inspire you. Think of the gifts of Eros, the god of love.

A Witch's Grimoire

[?] Use this time of enhanced psychic awareness to create a new moon esbat that deals with dreamwork. Write down your ideas for the new moon in Pisces esbat.

_____

_____

_____

7

Book of Transformation

There is a lady who weaves the night sky
Look at her fingers, she's flying so high
She is the Goddess who lives within
Our mother, our sister, our daughter, our friend
She changes everything she touches
And everything she touches changes
She changes everything she touches,
And everything she touches changes.
Changes, touches. Everything she touches changes.
Change is. Touch is. Everything she touches changes.
She is the weaver and we are the web
She is the needle and we are the thread.
She is the weaver and we are the web
She is the needle and we are the thread.
And she changes everything she touches
And everything she touches changes.
She changes everything she touches,
And everything she touches changes.
Changes, touches. Everything she touches changes.
Change is. Touch is. Everything she touches changes.

Witches throughout the world are familiar with this beloved chant, originated by the members of the Reclaiming tradition of Wicca, which illustrates the purpose of magic so beautifully. When we utter words of power, we are changed by those words. When we cast a spell, we are seeking to change the world around us for the greater good of all beings. When we cast a circle, we change a room or a grove into a sacred temple. When we build an altar, we change a table or other surface into the stage upon which deities and devotees interact. When we consecrate a tool, we change an ordinary item into an instrument of divine will. Change is the essence of magic, and we observe its effects all around us. The rising dawn changes night to day. Twilight changes day to night. Wind changes the face of the mountain. Rain changes the height of the river, which carves the valley and wears away the rock. Fire changes substance to ash. And the earth is a constantly shifting, spinning, revolving, and renewing planet. In this chapter, we explore the methods of magic that change our perception and how we interact with the world around us. These are the more advanced energies from which come the benefits of assiduous practice. This is the magic that changes us.

Trance: Traveling the Divine Matrix

While we previously explored the beneficial properties of meditation, trance work takes those basic techniques and builds on them to transport you further down the magical path. While the purpose of meditation is to quiet the mind and relax the body, trance work begins at the point where the effective meditation is actualized. In trance work, you are seeking not only mere relaxation, but also information and insight, even prophecy and a glimpse at things to come—images from the deep recesses of your mind.

Once a meditative state is achieved, it is possible to introduce ideas into the open and relaxed mind that will move the practitioner into a much deeper state of self-awareness. Because a trance can sometimes be difficult to control, it is important to verbalize what you are hoping to learn by allowing yourself to enter into a trancelike state. This is similar to the creative visualization, wherein you suspend disbelief and entertain imagination as reality. However, the trance differs in that the symbols and images you encounter will be generated by your own mind and not introduced into your consciousness by an outside source. A trance journey can be a very powerful experience, leading the practitioner to a deeper level of understanding of his or her own spirituality. It can illuminate the dark areas of the soul that we seek to embrace without fear. It can teach us why we choose the things that we do, why we seem to call in certain energies and not others.

Trance is a state of complete relaxation and trust as well as cognitive lucidity. In your meditative practice, you may have discovered the challenge of maintaining your energy level while simultaneously trying to relax. Maintaining lucidity is extremely important. A trance is not a nap or a daydream, but a concentrated effort to explore areas of the mind normally associated with dreaming while awake. Clarity will allow you to access the far corners of your mind. You may be surprised by what you discover there. Some people experience memories of a past existence. Others find a recurring problem illuminated in such as way as to achieve resolution. Some find inspiration through the removal of creative blockages.

Whatever your goal in entering a trancelike state, you will surely discover some dormant aspect of your mind or personality that will aid your magical workings. By committing your consciousness to traveling to a place beyond time, you are undertaking shamanic work, the work of the spiritual realm, and this is never to be taken lightly. You are, in essence, exploring the world of the deities, one that remains mostly hidden from us on the earthly plane of existence. How you experience this journey will be determined by your frame of mind. When you face the unknown with respect instead of fear, you open yourself to esoteric knowledge that would otherwise be unattainable.

A symbol often used in magic is that of the six-pointed star, composed of two overlapping triangles, one pointing up, one pointing down. Also known as the Star of David, this symbol, in addition to its association with Judaism, is regarded as the magical symbol for the upper world and the lower world: "as above, so below." It is a highly charged conduit for psychic intent. We seek knowledge of the world beyond while maintaining our connection to the earth. We seek communion with the spirits without having to permanently leave our bodies. We seek comprehension of the afterlife while we keep our life on earth. It is the line between these worlds that you are choosing to walk when you enter a trance. It is much more than something that can be conjured by your imagination alone. Your encounters along the paths between the worlds are powerful images.

One of the most immediate challenges you will face when beginning your trance work is letting go of intellectual reasoning. This is the voice that has you convinced that imagination is not reality and that experiences outside of the laws of reason are not to be trusted. You must first leave this voice behind.

TOOLS OF THE TRANCE

In classical Greece, the priestesses of Delphi were renowned for their oracular advice. The priestess would remain in the temple, seated above a crack in the earth from whence mysterious vapors would emanate. She inhaled these vapors and entered into a trance that enabled her to speak the words of the gods. People would travel for miles to hear the oracle's prophecy and to seek its counsel.

Similarly, European and other shamans use trance journeys to communicate with spirits and deities, both the spirits of nature as well as the spirits of those who have passed on to the afterlife. Although separated by continents and years, many cultures have used shamanic tools to aid their spiritual work.

Drumming is an effective tool to assist in developing and maintaining a trancelike state. Begin with a steady rhythm. Strike the drum in even, deliberate beats. You may also use rhythmic hand clapping, as this was an

Book of Transformation

effective method of invocation in ancient Egypt. If you do not own a drum, use a prerecorded drumbeat to assist you in developing your trance state. You can link the sound of the drum to your own heartbeat and to the pulse of life that is inherent in nature. Just as we learned earlier that speaking spells in rhyme and rhythm improves their effectiveness, so too does the drumbeat connect us to the universal life force. It is also a strong sound to focus on, allowing you to ignore distractions. Keeping the beat simple, steady, and strong will assist you in maintaining a trance.

Chanting is another method of rhythmically inducing a trance state. Instead of relying on a percussive instrument, you rely solely on the strength and power of your own voice. The chant can be a repeated mantra or a simple tune. If a musical chant is chosen, the chant should be of simple melody, varying by only a few notes. If the chant contains any words, they should be few and repetitive. You are not trying to put on a vocal performance, but using your voice as an instrument of change to connect your psyche with divine energies while discarding all distractions that may interfere with your ability to give yourself over to the trance. The chant is something to focus on while you commit to the act of releasing your inner being to divine consciousness. Once this commitment is felt by every part of your being, the chant will become second nature to you and may feel as natural and as unobtrusive as breathing.

In early Egypt as well as today, the sistrum is used as a highly effective trance-assisting tool. Like the drum, its ancient origins connect us to the spiral of humanity, and all those who have sought out greater knowledge of the spiritual realms. The sistrum is basically a rattle, often made of carved wood with metal clappers that create a sound as the sistrum is shaken. The sistrum also resonates with the rising power of Kundalini, whose energy is said to produce a rattle and a hiss as she uncoils herself and begins to rise through the chakras. When the sistrum is rocked back and forth in a steady motion, it gives the practitioner a strong focus and a tangible connection to ancient rituals. The rhythm is again the key to assisting the practitioner in maintaining the trance.

Dancing is another method employed in trance work. It can be as simple as a steady, swaying back-and-forth motion that evolves into increased energy as the trance deepens. In some cultures, physical exertion is an important aspect of developing the trance. It is believed that once the body reaches a point of exhaustion, the mind will be free to travel the astral planes without interference. While physical exhaustion may be unnecessary, developing a repetitive movement that is easy to execute will give you an anchor in this world while you travel in your mind to points beyond.

THE TRANCE JOURNEY

The trance is a mysterious journey of the spirit, sacred to the shaman, the magician, and the priestess alike. Most witches accept the concept of reincarnation just as readily as we accept the fact that the summer grass will rise again. Scientifically, we understand that matter can neither be created nor destroyed; it can only change from one form to another. When we create incense, we combine ingredients that exist in nature to make something that does not occur in nature. When we burn the incense, carbon ash remains where herbs and resins once were. Matter may undergo a permanent physical change, but it still exists in a completely different form. We relate this to the spiritual realm as evident in the soul of nature and the soul of humanity as well. All that dies will be reborn, in one form or another. We accept that there is a spiritual realm parallel to our own realm. Because these dimensions are parallel, they may coexist but seldom intersect. The purpose of a trance is to dance between these worlds, keeping a tie to one while exploring the other.

In Wicca, we often speak of "between the worlds," "the world above, and the world below." When you enter a trance, you may perceive these parallel realms as the earthly and the spiritual, the dominion of nature and the dominion of the goddesses and gods. One is a path ascending to the heavens.

Book of Transformation

The other is a tunnel into the secrets of the earth. As we live through the emotional heights and depths of our lives, we choose either consciously or unconsciously to send the spiral of our life up or down. So, too, in trance, do we decide whether to explore the world above or the world below. Keep in mind that there is no value judgment placed on these two aspects of the world beyond. Unlike the Christian concepts of heaven and hell, the spiritual realms of the witch are equal but opposite reflections of each other, free from predisposed positioning as exclusively good or evil and forbidden to some and not others.

1. Begin by using your most effective meditation technique.

2. Envision the path you will take slowly and deliberately. Start a trance-inducing rhythm. Let the rhythm be your guide. Choose your path and envision yourself circling around it slowly in a spiral.

3. Explore the limits of what your mind can create.

4. Close your eyes to eliminate visual distractions. Allow the dreams and visions to come.

Do not try to force an outcome, and do not try to interpret as you go. Open your mind and accept what occurs to you naturally.

Give yourself plenty of time and poetic license. Remember that trance is a journey and it is the path that the matters most, not the destination.

Scrying: Things That Are, That Were, That Shall Be

Scrying has much in common with trance, but it differs in that the tools used in scrying are physical objects rather than rhythmic techniques and also in that predictions are usually revealed to the practitioner visually as opposed to intuitively. This is not to imply that intuition is unnecessary, just that the information communicated to you during scrying will be interpreted primarily through visual clues rather than thoughts and feelings. The most important aspect of successful scrying is concentration. To gain the benefits of scrying, concentration must be earnestly cultivated and remain unbroken. Scrying is used to obtain information about a circumstance that would otherwise remain hidden. This can include knowledge, insight, or a glimpse into the future. Often, scrying will reveal three things: things that have already come to pass, things that are active in the present moment, and things that are yet to be. The accuracy of the past and present images will give you the sense of whether or not the future prophecy is a genuinely possible outcome. Only the scryer will be able to ascertain the truthfulness and the desirability of the omen. Always remember that because we are creatures who possess free will, no vision granted during a scrying session is carved in stone; rather, it is revealed through the mist, which is fluid and changeable. It is the individual witch who will affect her future the most, either by taking action or avoiding action. The path that we choose will have more impact on any outcome than mere portent. The purpose of seeking clarity in scrying is so that we can decide which path to take to bring about or circumvent the prediction as it is revealed.

THE CRYSTAL BALL

By far one of the most popular tools for scrying, the crystal ball has long been associated with predicting the future. Rarely is a fortuneteller, genuine or charlatan, portrayed without this magical tool. Genuine crystal balls are made by taking the "heart" of a large natural quartz crystal and polishing it into a sphere. While their inspiring beauty and inherent conductivity is unsurpassed, these crystals can be quite expensive and difficult to obtain. Often, they are filled with numerous natural inclusions, or visible pathways of the internal crystal matrix. Some witches find that the clearer the crystal,

Book of Transformation

the more useful it is for scrying. Others prefer the natural matrix of genuine quartz, as it lends itself easily to conjuring the mists. Leaded crystal is a more affordable alternative and provides an internally clearer orb. If clarity and affordability are your main requirements, you may wish to select an acrylic or Plexiglas ball. Visually, it will have much the same appearance as the leaded quartz, and though it is not made of natural material, it is very durable. Whatever type of crystal ball you choose, it is your concentration and the amount of energy that you put into it that will have the greatest impact on the success of your abilities than anything else.

1. Begin with a simple purification ritual, burning sage or incense or alternately using salt and water to banish unwanted influences.

2. Begin your meditative breathing exercises and prepare yourself for entering a trance-like state.

3. Place the crystal ball centered on your altar on a black cloth and sit comfortably before it, gazing into its center with concentrated effort. The cloth will prevent visual distractions from entering into your field of view.

4. It is so important to remain focused. Do not "zone out" and just stare at the crystal. Keep your eyes focused on the center and keep your mind attuned to the crystal. You must be an active participant in this process for it to work. You will soon know you are scrying correctly if the Goddess reveals a vision to you. Sometimes, a person will experience a glimpse of divine consciousness within the space of a few seconds. A vision or an omen may also manifest spontaneously. But often, the Goddess will not reveal an omen to someone who is not ready and prepared to receive it, just as pouring water into a covered jar will not fill the jar at all. Or alternately, a vision is granted but if the practitioner is unprepared, the meaning will be incomprehensible. The possibility of understanding the message will remain, but the

result may be elusive. You already posses the innate capacity, but whether or not you can open yourself to receiving the vision depends entirely on you.

5. Hone your powers of concentration. Look deep into the center of the crystal, holding your gaze steady without allowing your eyes to lose focus or glaze over. Blink whenever necessary so that you do not strain your eyes. Try limiting the amount of time you spend on each scrying session so that you do not become immersed and lose sight of reality.

6. Use this chant, or any portion of it, to aid your focus:

Crystal river crystal moon
Blackest night and brightest noon
By my breath and by my broom
Hearken to the witch's rune.
The mists of time may gather here
A thousand secrets to reveal
Mysteries to see and feel
Guided by the sacred wheel.
A question that I seek to know
As it is above, so be it below
Gentle as the candle's glow
May the vision start to grow.
What was, what is, or what will be
Show me what I need to see.
By all the power of three times three
As my will, so mote it be.

7. As you gaze into the crystal, it will seem to fill with mist. The mist will swirl and fill the ball, giving it a smoky appearance. As the mists slowly dissipate, a picture will be revealed to you. The picture may be still or mov-

ing, black and white or in color. Much like a dream, the image will most likely need some kind of interpretation. It could be a vision from the distant or recent past, the present, or the future.

8. Write down the image that you see in your book of shadows, including any specific details that occur to you. These may prove to contain useful insights when you go to interpret what you have seen.

OTHER SCRYING METHODS AND TOOLS

Another popular tool for scrying is the black mirror. You can easily make a scrying mirror by taking a concave piece of glass and covering the outside surface of it with black enamel. The result will be a dark and highly reflective tool. Like any other ritual tool, you should consecrate it before using it for magical purposes and keep it protected between scrying sessions. No one other than you should handle your scrying tools. When not in use, cover your tool with a cloth, preferably made of natural fiber, and keep it in a safe place. You may also modify the chant to suit your scrying tool of choice, as in this example:

Mirror, mirror dark as night
Grant to me your sacred sight
By the candle's gentle glow
Send me what I need to know
Reveal the secrets left unseen
In visions granted, like a dream
Of future, present or the past
Reflected in your darksome glass
Goddess bless the skills I hone
Blessed Maiden, Mother, Crone.
A mystery I wish to see
As I do will, so mote it be.

A Witch's Grimoire

You can also use a glass bowl filled with water for scrying. A dark type of glass such as obsidian or cobalt will work best, as it will provide better reflection. This is an excellent choice for witches who do intensive work with goddesses associated with water, such as Aphrodite (born from the sea), Brigid (one of her symbols is the well), Thetis (a Greek goddess of water), or Stella Maris (Star of the Sea).

You may find it more comfortable to hold a bowl of water and look down into it for the best results. Use a chant specific to the water element to aid your concentration:

Blessed water, pure and cool
Reflections in a sacred pool
Constant since the dawn of time
Ever changing and divine
Reveal the secrets of the dream
Mysteries that live unseen
Show the visions of the deep
So that your secrets I may keep
Future visions, present, past
What will fade and what will last
Goddess of the Star and Sea
Grant me what I ask of thee
By all the power of three times three
As I will so must it be.

Whatever method of scrying you choose, remember it is your level of concentration, your ability to clear your mind, and your ability to retain and interpret what you have seen that will determine your success. Keep records in your book of shadows to improve your experience with this technique by answering the following questions:

Book of Transformation

Scrying

Type of incense used during initial cleansing

___

___

Method and tools used (crystal, mirror, water, or other)

___

___

Lunar phase

___

___

Visions or images seen

___

___

Duration of scrying session

___

___

A Witch's Grimoire

Aspecting: The Goddess Reveals Her Many Faces

When we think of aspects of the Goddess, the three archetypes come to mind: the Maiden, the Mother, and the Crone. Meant to follow the blossoming and progression of womanhood through all stages of life, the Goddess in her triple aspect shows the feminine journey through life. While we primarily relate to this in terms of age and experience, the Triple Goddess is there to teach us that our entire journey through life is sacred, and each phase of womanhood is to be revered for different reasons. Each aspect represents a different level of knowledge and a different rite of passage.

No matter what stage of life a woman is in, she may alternately manifest any one of the aspects of the Triple Goddess at any given time. Some very young priestesses may demonstrate the knowledge and wisdom of the crone. A crone may radiate the energy and enthusiasm of the maiden. The mother aspect does not necessarily require an individual to be a biological mother; a witch may show the mother aspect in her work. All forms of nurturing represent the Goddess in her mother aspect, whether you are tending a garden, taking care of animals, or birthing a creative project.

Singular goddesses across diverse mythologies are often represented as the embodiment of many different characteristics within themselves, including phases of life or unique abilities. Consider the three aspects of the Irish goddess Brigid: She is the goddess of the forge, the patroness of silversmiths. She is also the keeper of the flame of inspiration, the creative fire, and manifests as the patroness of poets. Finally, she is also Brigid the healer. You can also gain understanding of the scope of the many aspects of the goddess by contemplating the Nine Muses of Greek mythology. Each individual muse is representative of a unique and specific expression:

- Thalia, muse of comedy
- Melpomene, muse of tragedy
- Terpsichore, muse of the dance

Book of Transformation

- Cleo, muse of heroic poetry
- Polyhymnia, muse of sacred songs
- Urania, muse of astronomy
- Euterpe, muse of lyric poetry
- Erato, muse of love poetry
- Calliope, muse of epic poetry

Aspects of the goddess are also represented by the phases of womanhood. The key to understanding the manifestation of the Goddess in her triple aspect is to first realize what your unique abilities and interests are, what phase of life you are currently in, regardless of your biological age, and then to realize that your life echoes of the aspects of the Goddess at once, just as surely as you still contain the essence of every age you have ever been. Even as you change and grow and, yes, age, you will still retain the essence of your present self.

Part of the beauty of what is referred to as *aspecting* involves entering a trancelike state and receiving a direct communication from the Goddess. This is most often facilitated by making an intimate connection with a particular manifestation of the Goddess and devoting yourself to learning all you can about her specific rituals, mythology, history, and symbolism. Many witches will feel drawn to a particular characteristic of a goddess for reasons that are difficult to articulate, but many will agree that the goddess archetypes inspire magic and empower the devotee, bringing added significance to the work. Getting in touch with a specific Goddess gives you a unique connection to her and a way of identifying the parts of yourself that you wish to make sacred through dedication to the divine. When you establish a clear and undeniable connection to a specific attribute of the Goddess, you will often find that she rewards her devotees abundantly. When invoked with sincerity, she will come to your aid. In your hour of need, your requests will be granted—although not necessarily in the manner in which you would expect. The Goddess is infinitely wise and directs the energy we send out to where it most needs to go. The more familiar you become with her and the more diligently you study this goddess, the more successful your work will be.

If you are already familiar with various attributes of the Goddess you want to work with (or who has selected you), use your book of shadows to deepen this connection by writing down her stories, myths, and legends. If you are new to discovering the Goddess of Ten Thousand names, the following list of twenty-two goddesses will assist you in gaining familiarity with what we might call a "global goddess."

Consider aspects of yourself that already resonate with the Goddess, for example, your ancestral heritage, geographical affinities, interests, and natural talents. The greater your self-knowledge, the more comfortable you will be with choosing your goddess.

The Goddess Known by Many Names

Goddess Name	Triple Aspect	Geographical Origin	Symbols and Titles
Aphrodite	Mother	Greece	Goddess of Love and Beauty, Most Beautiful, born from the Sea
Ariadne	Mother	Crete	Silver Thread, the Deep Sea, Guide of Souls through the Labyrinth

Book of Transformation

THE GODDESS KNOWN BY MANY NAMES

Artemis	Maiden	Greece	Moon Goddess, Virgin Goddess of the Hunt
Astarte	Mother	Greece	The Star, Goddess of Fertility and Love
Athena	Maiden	Greece	The White Owl, the Shield. Born from her father's head
Bast	Maiden	Egypt	Feline Goddess, Goddess of Beauty and Dance
Brigid	Mother	Ireland	Goddess of the Forge, Smithcraft, Healing, and Poetry
Cerridwen	Crone	Wales	The Cauldron, Goddess of Mysteries, Creation, and Inspiration

A Witch's Grimoire

THE GODDESS KNOWN BY MANY NAMES

Demeter	Mother	Greece	Grain, the Fruitful Earth, Mother to Persephone
Diana	Maiden	Rome	The Moon, Bow and Arrow, Mother of Aradia
Hathor	Maiden	Egypt	Crescent Moon, Cow Goddess
Hecate	Crone	Greece	The Cave, the cauldron, Wise Woman, Crone of Wisdom
Inanna	Mother	Sumer	Queen of Heaven, Goddess of Descent and Resurrection
Ishtar	Mother	Babylon	River of Life, Lady of Victory, King Maker
Isis	Mother	Egypt	Solar Disc, Crescent Moon, Throne, Mother of All Beings

Book of Transformation

The Goddess Known by Many Names

Kali	Crone	India	Destroyer of Illusions, Wearer of Skulls, Dances Upon the Burning Ground
Kwan Yin	Mother	China	Lotus, Goddess of Peace, Love, Compassion, and Mercy
Rhiannon	Maiden	Celtic	Goddess of Death and Rebirth, the Great Queen, Horse Goddess, with three birds she releases the living from life and resurrects the dead.
Sekhmet	Mother	Egypt	Lionheaded Goddess of Strength, Warrior Goddess
Tara	Mother	India, Tibet	Mother of All Activities, Goddess of Twenty-One Aspects

A Witch's Grimoire

Think about the many ways in which the Goddess has manifested through many ages and many lands as you complete the following questions to identify your goddess aspect.

[?] Phase of life you are currently in (your biological age)

_____

_____

[?] Biological age you feel most attuned to (Ex: "I'm forty going on seventeen!")

_____

_____

[?] Ancestral heritage and family origin, including significant migrations

_____

_____

[?] Interests and hobbies that come naturally to you

_____

_____

[?] Abilities you have developed through discipline

_____

_____

Book of Transformation

{ ? } Symbols and images that you are instinctively drawn to

_____

_____

Channeling: The Goddess Speaks Through You

While channeling is considered to be a very advanced practice, by its nature it is also passive. It takes a good measure of trust and confidence to allow yourself to become a channel for spiritual energy. During channeling, the channel or medium opens herself to directly and deliberately receiving the divine presence of another entity—deity or discarnate spirit or dead person—into her body. This is usually only achieved after many years of constant attunement, meditative practice, and highly developed focus. To channel the energy of the Goddess is to serve as her oracle, to actually let the words of other entities flow through you and speak through you. In order to channel effectively, you must have a finely tuned connection to the other world. An oracle will not manifest uninvited, and the amount of sincerity, faith, and focus with which you craft your invocation can make all the difference in your ability to channel.

An excellent preparation for channeling first involves learning all you can about the energy of the Goddess you wish to channel. If you have a personal affinity for her, now is the time to delve deeper and do your research. Familiarize yourself with her ancient rites and come up with parallels relating to modern day. Learn her mythology by heart so that it becomes second nature to you. Read books about her. Gather any archaeological facts and information that increase your knowledge of the specific nature of her worship. Find out how she was honored in the past, what names her devotees used to invoke her presence, and what her favorite offerings were. Keep records and notes of your research in your book of shadows and reread them frequently until they are engraved in your mind. Craft thorough and sincere invocations to the Goddess with whom you wish to communicate. The Goddess will show herself in the manifestation of aspect through the divine name that she is called upon.

Developing the gift of channeling is a great privilege, a gift that once resulted in the hanging or burning of women (and some men) who employed this power. Approach your work with reverence. It is not likely that you will be able to channel on command. Only on very rare occasions does the total identification with the deity take place. You can greatly enhance your abilities through gaining knowledge and ritual experience. Commit to memory oracles that have been written by the ancients and handed down. Practice reciting them so that you are comfortable with your own voice and gain confidence speaking aloud. This will enable you to avoid fumbling for words if you are able to channel an original oracle. Invoke the goddess with humility. Remember that the divine essence permeates all beings, and although you are an essential part of this divine matrix, you do not control it. Seek truth through inspiration and commit your total consciousness to receiving the oracle.

When the Goddess is effectively invoked, she does not merely announce, "Here I am!" She will make her true self known to you through symbol, image, and myth, and she will most often have a message to impart. It is no accident that you feel called to a certain aspect of the Goddess, for each of us is a child of the Goddess and it is only a matter of time before we realize this. This is an attainable and desirable endeavor, and with focus, reverence, sincerity, humility, and devotion, you may soon find yourself transcribing into your book of shadows oracles that have been bestowed to you directly from the Goddess. Use the following guide to assist you in developing techniques that will lead you to successful channeling:

Book of Transformation

Preparation. This includes a consistent meditative practice. You must prepare yourself and your sacred space.

Research. Learn all you can about the deity or spirit you wish to invoke. Familiarize yourself with ancient rites of worship and relate those to your modern-day experience.

Invocation. Your original invocation will include specific references to the Goddess you wish to invoke, as well as your reasons for calling upon her. What is it, exactly, that you are hoping to accomplish? Whether you are seeking esoteric knowledge, inspiration, or abundance, your invocation must include your statement of intent.

Channeling. When the Goddess speaks through you, you may find that words and visions flow freely as a wild river, carrying you to places unimaginable. Try to accept this energy and retain the experience of receiving communication from the deities by writing down the images as they occur to you. You will often find that an oracle will have a specific message that relates to your immediate experience. Recording as many details as you are able will allow you to deepen your understanding of what has transpired.

8

Book of Lights and Shadows

Day and night. Sun and moon. Above and below. These are just three examples of the polarity in nature as reflected through the Craft of the Wise. Lights and shadows have equal lessons to teach. It is prudent to listen to and observe the wisdom of the forces of nature if we ever hope to understand and align ourselves with them and benefit from this alliance. Move into the light and feel its inspiration. Embrace the darkness and welcome its mystery. Find yourself within the spiral matrix of creation and make your mark. Write your dreams and your fears. Write your aspirations and your desires. Get to know yourself as a spiritual being, a reflection of the Goddess. Embrace your individuality while recognizing your connection to all: all of life, the fabric of nature, the void of space, the rocks, the trees, and the creatures that dwell on land, in the sea, and fly through the air. Deepen yourself into your craft. Remember that an empowering aspect of Wicca lies in your actions, not simply in your thoughts, intentions, and words. While it is advantageous to learn all you can, how you use the knowledge you have accumulated will be the true measure of your journey. Keeping your book of shadows will be one of your most valuable tasks on this journey. Remember where you have been, and look to the future as you create and learn, change, and grow.

Candle Magic

It is easy to see why, since our foremothers found fire, it has held such great significance. To our earliest ancestors who lived in caves and relied solely on their strength for their continued existence, fire was nothing less than the key to survival. Fires were built in caves for protection. They kept predators away, heated caves, and cooked foods.

As early civilizations worshiped the sun, fire was no less than the embodiment of deity on earth. In classical Greece, the tale of Prometheus illustrates this bond. Prometheus, a mortal man, was said to have stolen the sacred fire from Zeus on Mount Olympus and brought it to humankind. The price of his theft was worse than death. As punishment, Zeus had him chained to a rock where an eagle tore out his liver every day. Every night, his body was regenerated so that the torture could begin again the next day.

When a candle is consecrated to a magical purpose, it is infused with intention and thereby transformed from a material object into a catalyst for change. Action changes the mundane into the magical. The candle is lit, and linked to the gods. Thought is bound to intention, and intention is bound to deed. As the wick burns, wax is consumed and unites with the atmosphere, symbolic of the power of the gods touching and changing the material world. Physical change is readily observed, and psychic change is believed to take effect. The power of the deities releases our intentions into the universe, where the gods deliver them to their rightful consequence so that the best possible outcome may manifest.

Candle burning is observed in nearly all religions. In Wicca, it has particular importance in that the preparation, dedication, and implementation of the magic are done by each practitioner according to her will. More important, it is a highly regarded practice because candle magic works. The benefits are almost immediately observed, and although outcomes may not manifest in quite the manner in which the individual may have expected, undeniable results are nonetheless quite common and should rightly be anticipated.

The type of candle that you choose should reflect the work you intend to do. Taper candles, votive candles, jar candles, and image candles are commonly used, according to your desire. After choosing the type of candle that suits your needs, the next aspect to consider is the candle's color. Each color has its unique vibration and associations, and you want to be sure that you are making the best possible choice for the work at hand. Consider the following list when making your selection:

White candles are recommended for meditation, divination, lunar magic, spells that involve communicating with spirits, and petitions for healing. White is symbolic of purity, and burning a white candle denotes spiritual strength, seeking the truth, and the attainment of peace.

Black candles are often burned during banishing rituals. Also used for uncrossing and meditation, black candles in ritual are often charged to repel negativity.

Blue candles are used to invoke prophetic dreams and general protection while sleeping. Since blue is widely associated with soothing and calming energies, blue candles also signify tranquility, loyalty, and peace.

Red candles are often burned during spells for love, attraction, fertility, health, vigor, strength, courage, and willpower.

Yellow candles enhance studiousness, as the color yellow is associated with wisdom and confidence. Yellow candles are also related to persuasion and charm.

Green candles are used in spells for fertility, new growth, good luck, success, and prosperity.

Purple candles are used for the manifestation of psychic awareness, power, independence, and protection of the household.

Orange candles are used in spells to stimulate energy, end fallow periods, and remove psychic barriers.

Brown candles are used for grounding energy, improving concentration, and for the protection of animal familiar spirits and household pets. Brown candles are also used in spells for finding lost objects.

Silver candles are burned in rituals to attune with lunar energy, restore stability, and honor the Goddess.

Gold candles are burned in rituals to attune with solar energy, god energy, and to attract the power of the cosmos.

This list is intended as a guide, and not a substitution for originality or inspiration. Trust your instincts. Record your candle spells in your book of shadows and you will have a better sense of what works best for you.

After choosing your candle, the next step is consecrating and dressing the candle. This is the preparation for the magical work. It is at this stage that you will state your intention and imbue that intention into the candle. Consider the following questions:

Book of Lights and Shadows

- What is it that you hope to change, or most wish to achieve?
- Is this desire in line with the tenets of Wicca, in that it will harm none and will be of benefit to all beings?
- How do you foresee the outcome of your intention coming into place?

1. Name your intention and meditate upon it until it is as clear as a candle's flame.

2. Hold the candle in your hand and close your eyes. Visualize your thoughts permeating the wax and being contained within the candle itself.

3. Carve symbols that represent your intentions into the wax. You may use your bolline, a small wooden stick or toothpick, or a nail or pin. Some things you will want to consider carving into the candle are runes, insignias, astrological symbols, planetary symbols, elemental symbols, names, and dates. Select the symbols that most highly resonate with your work beforehand and practice them in your book of shadows. In candle carving, there is no erasing. Do not, however, become overly concerned with the artistic renderings of symbols. It is your intention that is the most important aspect of this work, and not whether you draw well. The magic is in the doing of the task.

4. Once you have completed the carving of your candle, anoint it with an essential oil that will also resonate with your work. Apply the oil to the middle of the candle and then work it gradually in each direction to balance the polarity of the two ends—as above, so below. Think of your petition or intention rising up to the heavens as you anoint the top of the candle upward, and then bring the completed work down to reality on earth as you anoint the bottom of the candle.

5. Let the oil seep into the carvings and coat the candle in a thin, even layer. Dress the candle further by applying incense or even glitter to accentuate the carvings. The oil will make it easy for the dressing material to adhere to the candle's surface and will also make its appearance pleasing.

6. Next, make an offering to the Goddess to bless your work and align your personal energy with the candle. Take a drop of honey and place it on the fleshy part of your hand where the thumb meets the palm. Take another drop of honey and place it on the bottom of the jar or candle holder that you wish to use. As you place the candle in its jar or holder, simultaneously lick the honey from your hand. If you are using a jar candle with a removable candle, you can even sprinkle a little incense and place three pennies in the bottom of the jar to accentuate the conductive energy and as an offering to the Triple Goddess. If the candle is nonremovable, place the incense and pennies under the jar itself.

7. You may speak the following charm to bind the spell to the candle, or improvise your own, substituting your specific intention where blank spaces are left:

Blessed be thou creature of wax
By the art of the hand you were made
By magic be now changed.
Thou art no more a candle, but [state your intention]
Blessed by the sweetness of the Goddess
Consecrated by my will and hand
Bound to this charge
For strengthening the greater good
For manifesting intention on earth
As an agent of the power of the Goddess
Charged with the power of three times three
As I will, so mote it be.

How you choose to burn your candle will be determined by the nature of the spell you are doing. Some candles should be burned completely and without interruption. Others may be burned for an hour every day at a specific time. Use your knowledge and intuition and remember never to leave a burning candle unattended. If you want to burn your candle without interruption but need to leave your altar, consider placing the candle in the fireplace with the screen closed or in the center of your bathtub with the shower curtain removed. But do this only if you do not have rambunctious pets that will be tempted to investigate, knock over, or otherwise interfere with what we know to be a potentially highly destructive element.

The Ritual Use of Herbs

While many herbs have medicinal and healing properties, for our purposes, we will focus on the metaphysical attributes of herbs.

Today, an herb is commonly defined as a perennial flowering plant, usually with a woody stem, that produces flowers, an aroma, and may contain healing properties. The earliest known herbal reference was written 5,000 years ago in China by the emperor Shen Nung. While the original text no longer exists, the proof lies in the influences found in many later herbals. Some 2,000 years before the birth of Christ, the Egyptians and Sumerians kept records regarding the use of herbs. Egyptians used herbs primarily for cosmetic, medicinal, and embalming purposes. As the Mediterranean trade routes grew and flourished, the use of herbs spread to Greece. Hippocrates, the legendary doctor, included in his writings roughly 400 herbal remedies. His remedies reflected his belief that all illness and disease was caused by imbalances in the four bodily humours, which reflect the four elements of earth, water, fire, and air. Herbal remedies were recommended for correcting these physical imbalances to facilitate healing. In ancient Britain, the Druidic priests, who were also healers, sought after astrological knowledge and combined planetary influences with mysticism and practicality through the use of herbs.

Herbs may be gathered or procured in numerous ways. Herbs grown naturally without the assistance or interference of an outside source such as a gardener or farmer are referred to as *wildcrafted*. These herbs, prized because of their wild nature, are harvested in their maturity. Though cultivated herbs are grown in a controlled environment, they can be just as effective and potent as wild herbs. There is a special relationship that develops between the plants and the person tending to them, so if you do not live in an area where you can find wild herbs, consider growing your own in a pot garden or windowbox. Herbs can also be purchased fresh, dried, or in bulk from most green grocers and farmers' markets.

When selecting herbs, make sure they are full of vitality. Look for signs of wilting or sun damage. If you are purchasing your herbs and do not know under what conditions they were grown, make sure you wash them thoroughly to remove any residual chemicals that may have been used during the growing period and are possibly still present. When you grow or find and harvest or gather your own herbs, you will need a knife, a trowel, and possibly a root digger. Make sure you ask permission from the herb before taking it from its original growth area. Also leave an offering such as a poured libation or a small crystal to honor the earth. Look around and see if the surrounding environment is free from litter or other debris. Try to leave your surroundings better than you found them for the sake of the plants and out of respect for the earth.

When you bring your herb harvest—gathered or purchased—home with you, the next step is drying the herbs properly so that they will retain as much of their life force as possible so that it may be released later when you have need of it. The best way to dry herbs is by hanging them upside down in bunches in a cool, dry, relatively dark place. Sunlight is very powerful and will quickly deteriorate the herbs. You can see sun damage in drying herbs if they lose their color and fade to pale yellow. You can also dry the herbs flat by spreading them out on a plate or cutting board wrapped in cloth. If you choose the flat drying method, you will need to turn the herbs frequently so that they dry evenly and do not rot.

Once you have dried the herbs, you can either leave them hanging in bunches or remove the leaves and flowers and store them in airtight jars or bottles made of dark glass. This slows the damaging effects of light and will preserve the herbs for a longer period of time. The best colors for dried herb storage jars are amber and cobalt.

Harvested herbs, whether fresh or dried, can be prepared and used for magical purposes in numerous ways. An herbal infusion can be made by boiling water, removing the water from heat, and then adding the herbs to steep for several minutes. Herbs with thick woody stems need to be decocted; that is, boiled directly in the water for a short period of time and then strained.

Essential oils can also be prepared from herbs. Oils are used in magic in a variety of ways, most notably for anointing, consecrating, and blessing. Each different type of oil, like each herb that it is derived from, has its unique associations that enhance the power of the spell, the sacredness of an object, or the will of the practitioner.

Another useful herbal preparation is flower water. Flower water is made from fresh herbs whose essence is captured in water and preserved with a tiny amount of liquor such as brandy or vodka. Flower waters can be used as an asperge to purify a room, to charge an amulet for a ritual or spell, or even worn on the body as a scent.

Herbal preparations that contain only one herbal ingredient are referred to as simples, whereas a blended mixture can be prepared by combining two or three different types of herbal preparations. Usually, a sacred oil mixture will contain at least a combination of two essential oils. These can be described as the base note and the top note. The base note is often earthy and based on the scent of a woody herb, while the top note is usually from a flowering herb. For example, a blended oil made from combined amounts of sandalwood, rose, and jasmine was considered sacred to Ishtar by the Babylonians.

Dried herbs can be tied in small bundles and hung in doorways or worn as charms, or crumbled together in a mixture and sewn up in a sachet or pillow. Different colors of embroidery thread, cord, ribbon, and cloth can be used to lend effectiveness to the herbal charm. Consider how the energies of different colors can enhance the many ways of preparing herbal charms. Colored ribbon or thread can be used to tie the herbs in small bundles like a bouquet, or the herbs can be wrapped like a smudge stick. A piece of cloth can be cut into a circle or a square, the herbs placed in the center, and the ends of cloth gathered together and tied securely. You can also choose colors with intention to complement your desired result. Use a specific color cloth and perhaps a different color thread if you want to sew a pillow or sachet. Refer to the following list to assist you in making your color choices.

Blue is associated with calming properties and invokes peace and tranquility.

Purple can be used to promote psychic awareness and communication with higher powers.

Turquoise is often used for enhancing friendships.

Green is suitable for charms intended to bring about positive growth and healing. It can be used when expansion, change, or movement is required.

Yellow may be used when the purpose of the charm is to enhance mental acuity, clarity, and foresight.

Orange can be used to denote physical pleasure and sexuality.

Pink promotes love and romance.

Red is associated with vitality and victory.

Silver can be used for herbal charms that deal with lunar magic, or when you wish to reflect a certain energy that has been directed at you; it is also used to improve safety during travel.

Gold can be used for herbal charms that deal with solar magic, prosperity, and attainment.

Brown would be a good choice for earth magic or for grounding energy. Brown is also used for charms to find a home.

White denotes purity, spirituality, and light. White is also used for sending energy outward.

Black is used for absorbing and grounding energy. It is also effective for reversing unwanted energy that has been directed toward you.

1. Before using dried herbs for a magical purpose, spread them out in front of you, either on a clean plate or a counter top.

2. Project your intention into the herbs as you hold your hands directly over them. Concentrate on your wishes being fulfilled, your desires being granted.

3. With your index finger, draw a symbol that signifies your intention into the herbs. It could be a heart for invoking love, or a pentacle for protection, an ankh for longevity, or a caduceus for health.

A Witch's Grimoire

4. Visualize the best possible outcome for the benefit of all beings as you imbue the herbs with your energy.

Your herbs are now ready to use as you will, in a charm, sachet, infusion, or other fitting method. While herbs are natural substances, they are very potent and can also be dangerous. Many herbs are poisonous and should never be ingested. Essential oils are highly concentrated and can be irritating to the skin and eyes. Always consult a reputable herbal reference if you are considering using any herbal preparation internally or externally. Following are some of the metaphysical properties of commonly used herbs.

Allspice (*Pimenta officinalis*) is connected to the element of earth and is ruled by the planet Jupiter. Its attributes include healing properties as well as attracting money and prosperity.

Anise (*Pimpinella anisum*) is connected to the element of air and is ruled by Jupiter. Anise is used for promoting love and establishing relationships.

Basil (*Ocimum basilicum*) is associated with the element of fire and is ruled by Mars. Its magical uses include protection, attracting love and money, and inspiring fidelity.

Bay (*Laurus nobilis*) is associated with nobility and was often associated with the deities of Greece and Rome. Bay laurel was used by the ancient Greeks to crown the Olympic victors. Ruled by the sun, bay represents the element of fire and is used for enhancing psychic awareness, healing, purification, and protection. A bay leaf discovered in a dish while eating is considered good luck.

Book of Lights and Shadows

Black Pepper (*Piper nigrum*) is also ruled by Mars and associated with elemental fire. Its magical properties include protection and purification.

Caraway (*Elletaria cardamomum*) is associated with elemental water and is ruled by Venus. When its seeds are crushed, it emanates a beautiful scent that is said to inspire love and increase sexual desire.

Chamomile (*Chamaemelum nobile*), associated with the properties of fire and earth, is a very calming, soothing herb. It can be used in a ritual bath to promote emotional stability and peace.

Cinnamon (*Cinnamomum zeylanicum*) is ruled by the influence of the sun and represents the element of fire. Its metaphysical properties include enhancing psychic awareness and attracting love and money. Cinnamon was used as an offering to the deities in ancient Egypt.

Clove (*Syzygium aromatium, Caryophyllus aromaticus*) is considered sacred to the goddess Hecate. Ruled by Jupiter and associated with elemental fire, clove is said to bring about love, money, and protection.

Cumin (*Cuminum cyminum*) was worn around the neck as a protective charm in ancient Greece and was also used as a divine offering by the Egyptians. Cumin is ruled by Mars and associated with elemental fire. It is said to invoke peace and happiness.

Dandelion Blossom Oil

This is a basic flower oil recipe that can be used for anointing candles and talismans (used for enhancing psychic awareness) or any of the other associative metaphysical properties of dandelion. It is an excellent starting point for experimenting with making your own flower oil, as dandelions are weeds and grow abundantly in many parts of the world without special cultivation requirements. You may use this basic recipe and substitute different types of aromatic flowers that would be more attuned to the magical working you wish to accomplish.

Materials Needed

- Mixing cup
- Jar with a tight lid
- 1 chopstick
- Cold-pressed olive oil (amount determined by size of jar)
- Grapeseed oil (amount determined by size of jar)
- Dandelion blossoms

1. The dandelions should be gathered at high noon on a sunny day. This imbues them magically with the radiant energy of the sun, and for practical purposes, ensures that the blossoms will be dry.

2. Fill your jar completely with the blossoms and in a separate cup, combine equal amounts of the olive oil and grapeseed oil. You will need enough oil to completely fill the jar.

3. Pour the oil over the blossoms and use the chopstick to press out the air bubbles.

4. Place the cap on the jar and label it with the name and date. Keep the jar in a cool, dry area, since warmth will cause the dandelions to spoil.

5. For the first two weeks, you will need to open the jar every few days to press out the air bubbles and refill the jar with oil up to the top, making sure that afterward, the lid is tightly closed.

6. After six weeks, you can decant the oil into a pretty bottle or other container and use it for your spells and charms.

Dandelion (*Taraxacum officinale*) is associated with elemental air and is ruled by Jupiter. It is used to increase psychic awareness, inspire loyalty, prevent resentment, and balance anger.

Elder Flower Water

Elder flower water can be made simply and used as a magical potion for strengthening intuition.

Materials Needed

- Elder blossoms
- 1 half-gallon jar
- Boiled water
- 1½ ounces of liquor, either brandy or vodka

1. Elder blossoms are best gathered on Midsummer's Eve or a full moon, preferably in June. Fill your jar completely with the elder blossoms and pour the boiled water over them.

2. Add the liquor and allow the mixture to steep for several hours.

3. After the blossoms have steeped, strain them through cheesecloth and keep the water stored in a pretty bottle. Your potion is now ready for use. As you learn to create your own flower waters, you may experiment with different kinds of flowers. Keep records in your grimoire as you create your own original recipes.

Elder (*Sambucus nigra*) has long been regarded as a magical and holy tree. Its stems were worn as protective amulets to bring about health and good luck. Elder trees were often planted close to houses due to the belief that elder would never be struck by lightning. Elder blossoms, berries, and leaves were hung over doorways to drive away unwelcome spirits and to discourage thieves.

Book of Lights and Shadows

Dill (*Anethum graveolens*) is ruled by Mercury, the planet of intelligence. It is associated with elemental fire and is used to open the conscious mind and attract money. Europeans believed dill offered protection against evil, and it was even placed in wedding bouquets to bestow good luck.

Fennel (*Foeniculum vulgare*) is used for increasing physical and emotional strength. Also associated with protective energies, fennel is ruled by Mercury and is associated with elemental fire.

Garlic (*Allium sativum*) has been used in a wide assortment of magical purposes across many cultures. Eastern European lore connects garlic with protection against vampires, while Roman soldiers wore garlic to inspire courage in battle. These uses lend garlic its metaphysical properties of encouraging good health and providing protection. Ruled by Mars, garlic is associated with elemental fire.

Ginger (*Zingiber officinale*) originated in Asia and was used to communicate with deities and as an offering for the dead. In China, ginger was hung over the doorways of laboring mothers, as it was believed to protect mother and baby during childbirth. Ruled by Mars and associated with elemental fire, ginger is used magically to attract love and money. Ginger is also can also accelerate the results of spellwork.

Hawthorn (*Crataegus oxyacantha*) is the sacred herald of Beltane. Regarded as a highly magical tree, hawthorn blossoms are believed to bestow protective and visionary powers. Since the wood of the hawthorn tree is a very fine grain, it is ideal for carving magical talismans.

Lavender Bath Salts

To experience and appreciate lavender's lovely essence, try the following simple recipe for lavender bath salts.

Materials Needed

- Equal parts of Epsom salts, borax, and sea salt
- Mixing bowl
- Lavender essential oil

1. In a mixing bowl, combine the three salts and mix them together thoroughly.

2. Add several drops of lavender essential oil to the salts and sift them together. Let the mixture sit a while before you decide to add additional drops of oil. The oil will permeate the salts gradually, and you may not need as much lavender oil as you might think.

3. Store the salts in a pouch or jar and add them to your bathwater as a beautiful ingredient to a ritual bath.

Lavender (*Lavandula officinalis*) has long been regarded as a woman's herb. It is used to calm anxieties and contains great influence over emotions. Lavender is believed to inspire courage when undergoing a difficult transition or treading a painful path. For this reason, it is often used to soothe women during childbirth. Lavender is also a clarifying herb as well as an herb of beauty.

Book of Lights and Shadows

Licorice (*Glycyrrhiza glabra*) is used for attracting love and increasing sexual desire. Licorice is ruled by Venus and elemental water. A licorice charm can be made by tying two pieces of the root together with some red embroidery thread or yarn. This is thought to give protection against negativity and injuries.

Mandrake (*Atropa mandragora*) is regarded as a highly magical herb. Many species of plants that are referred to as mandrake, the American May apple being one of them. Mandrakes were prized for their magical potency because the root of the herb very strongly resembles the human form. It was believed that if a mandrake was pulled up from the ground, the plant would shriek so terribly that it would drive the harvester mad. It was a common medieval practice to loosen the earth around the mandrake, tie a string to the plant, tie the other end of the string to a hungry dog, and then hurl a piece of meat away from the animal so the dog would be the one actually uprooting the mandrake. Mandrake is a poisonous herb so it should never be ingested.

Marigold (*Calendula officinalis*) is ruled by the sun and elemental fire. It is said to invoke happiness and provide protection. Regarded in medieval times as one of the seven herbs of great virtue, marigold and a wolf's tooth wrapped together in a bay leaf, worn on one's person, was believed to stop slander and bring forth the respect of others. If a person had been robbed, this same charm left under a pillow during sleep was said to reveal the identity of the thief.

Marjoram (*Origanum marjorana*) was grown in the gardens of ancient Greece and Rome. As an omen, flourishing and thriving marjoram was an indication that the gardener would be prosperous. Failure to thrive signified financial ruin. Ruled by Mercury and associated with elemental air, this herb's magical properties include invoking love and peace.

Mugwort Dream Pillow

Because of its associations with the moon and psychic visions, mugwort can be used as a dream enhancer. It can inspire more vivid dreams and aid in dream recollection.

Materials Needed

- 2 rectangular pieces of blue or purple cotton cloth
- Needle and thread
- Dried mugwort leaves
- Dried lavender blossoms
- Pinch of mint
- 2 to 3 cups of flax seeds

1. Sew together on three sides two rectangular pieces of blue or purple cotton cloth.

2. Turn the cloth inside out and fill with the dried herbs. The mugwort will induce psychic dreams, while the lavender will have a calming effect. The touch of mint is for mental clarity. Fill the remainder of the pillow with the flax seeds and sew up the final side.

3. Sleep with the pillow and allow it to affect your dreams. Use your book of shadows to record any significant results.

Mugwort (*Artemisia vulgaris*), nicknamed cronewort, is considered sacred to the moon goddess Artemis because of the silvery color of the underside of its leaves. Mugwort symbolizes the gifts of vitality and freedom from repression. It is also used for centering, grounding, and the renewal of strength. When burned in small bundles, mugwort enhances psychic visions.

Mustard (*Brassica spp.*) is ruled by the planet Mars and associated with elemental fire. Carrying mustard seeds in a small pouch is thought to act as a guard against accidents. Its magical properties include protection and enhancing courage.

Nutmeg (*Myristica fragrans*) is ruled by Jupiter and associated with fire. Nutmeg is also used magically to augment psychic awareness. A whole nutmeg carried in the pocket is said to absorb negative vibrations while sending out positive vibrations.

Oregano (*Origanum vulgare*) is ruled by Mercury and associated with elemental air. Oregano is used to promote stability in relationships and to invoke peace.

Parsley (*Petroselinum sativum*) is used as a garnish today, but its origins are in ancient magic. Parsley was thought to ward off evil and was also considered sacred to the dead. Often, an offering of parsley was left as an honorable tribute to the animal that gave its life so that a family could have a meal. Ruled by Mercury and associated with elemental air, parsley is used for money drawing, protection, and attraction.

Peppermint (*Mentha piperita*) is ruled by the planet Mercury and is associated with elemental air. Peppermint's magical uses include purification, healing, and enhancing desire.

Pine (*Pinus albus*), in evergreen form, has long been honored as an emblem of immortality. Its ability to thrive in the cold of winter when other plants die off has reinforced its connotation as a symbol of enduring life. Magically, pine resin is burned to deflect and ward off negative influences. It is also regarded as a confidence builder.

To make pine oil suitable for anointing, infuse fresh pine needles in olive oil and seal in a jar for six weeks.

Poppy (*Papaver spp.*) is sacred to the goddesses Demeter and Ceres. Its magical connotations are fertility and love. Ruled by the moon, poppies are associated with elemental water.

Rose (*Rosa spp.*) is associated so closely with love that it is no coincidence that this plant is ruled by Venus. Associated with elemental water, roses are thought to bring comfort and cleansing.

Rosemary (*Rosemarinus officinalis*) is sacred to Venus and was considered to be the flower of Mount Olympus. It was often used in ceremonial magic in ancient Greece. Rosemary is thought to enhance the conscious mind and to promote healing and love. It is also used as a potent protection charm and for augmenting mental faculties.

Saffron (*Crocus sativus*) was considered sacred to the ancient Phoenicians and was used as an offering to the goddess Ashtoreth. Its magical properties include bringing happiness and enhancing spirituality. Since it is one of the rarest and most expensive of all herbs, it is used only sparingly in cooking. Ruled by the sun, saffron is connected to elemental fire.

Sage (*Salvia officinalis*) has been used in magic for more than 2,000 years, and is dedicated to Zeus in Greece and Jupiter in Rome. Long associated with longevity and health, sage is also said to bring wisdom and is considered a protector. When the leaves are crushed between the fingers, the scent is believed to increase mental agility. Magically, sage is used to attract money and manifest wishes. Sage is also the main component of the smudge stick, used to clear sacred space in preparation for ritual.

Thyme (*Thymus vulgaris*) is ruled by Venus and associated with the water element. Thyme was used for cleansing temples in ancient Greece, and is now used magically for purification, increasing psychic awareness, and attracting love. It is also used as incense for purifying the air and as a house blessing. To calm the nerves and banish nightmares, make an herb pillow filled with thyme. To calm your emotions and get in touch with yourself, try infusing a bath with thyme. Take two cups of dried thyme and sprinkle into two quarts of boiling water. Cover the pot and allow it to steep over the flame for approximately ten minutes. Strain out the herbs and add the extract to your bath water. Light a blue candle and soak yourself for fifteen minutes.

Turmeric (*Curcuma domestica*) can be mixed with seawater and used as an asperge to banish unwanted influences. Ruled by Mercury and associated with elemental air, turmeric's magical use is for purification.

Vanilla (*Vanilla planifolia*) is a delightful herb associated with love and sexuality. Its mythological origins are in Mexico, where the daughter of a fertility goddess fell in love with a mortal youth. Because of her status as a deity, she was unable to join with the object of her affection, and so transformed herself into the vanilla-bearing orchid flower so that she would still bring happiness and joy to her beloved.

Violet (*Viola tricolor, Viola odorata*), regarded as the plant of compassion, is also called "heart's ease." Violet's magical associations are

A Witch's Grimoire

the restoration of comfort and the easing of grief. Violet awakens the maiden aspect of the Goddess, opens the mind to psychic visions, and mends the wounded heart. To make a soothing violet mist, take a dropperful of violet leaf extract and a dropperful of violet blossom extract. Add the extracts to four ounces of natural spring water and pour into an atomizer. The violet mist can be sprayed on the face and neck as well as the heart.

Yarrow (*Achillea millefolium*), sacred to Venus, was used to ease restlessness, while its flowers provided psychic protection. The ancient oracle of China known as the I Ching was originally cast with yarrow stalks, lending great significance to the magical properties of this herb. Yarrow flowers sewn up in a sachet and placed under a pillow were thought to give the dreamer a glimpse of his or her future wife or husband when accompanied by this chant:

Thou pretty herb of Venus tree, thy true name is yarrow.
Now who my bosom friend must be, pray tell me tomorrow.

Herbs are highly potent magical ingredients. No doubt they will prove to be an essential element to your magical work. Use the following worksheet to keep records of your spells that use herbs so that you may continue to learn from these energetically charged gifts from the earth.

Book of Lights and Shadows

Spells with Herbs

Present situation

_____

_____

Desired change or effect

_____

_____

Herbs chosen (indicate if a simple or a blend is used)

_____

_____

Manner of preparation (infusion, oil, sachet, etc.)

_____

_____

Colors used (if any)

_____

_____

A Witch's Grimoire

Planetary influences

_____

_____

Phase of moon during spellwork

_____

_____

Results observed

_____

_____

Time elapsed

_____

_____

Book of Lights and Shadows

Sympathetic Magic and the Use of Gems

The basic philosophy of sympathetic magic is quite simple. It is believed that "like cures like." This philosophy is also used in homeopathy, in which the nature of a remedy has similar characteristics to the ailment it is prescribed to assuage. Likewise, in modern medicine, vaccination involves injecting healthy people with minute amounts of a usually inactive (although sometimes active in certain vaccinations) virus so that the body develops appropriate antibodies.

In sympathetic magic, we acknowledge that the inherent similarities between certain objects and colors is more than coincidental. We believe that these entities are linked on the spiritual plane, and by practicing magic, we enhance these associations to make spells more effective. What may seem like the exploration of extended metaphor is actually just common sense. Green candles are often used for money spells because U.S. currency is green on one side and because green denotes new growth—similar to new leaves that flourish. These are powerful associations. Thought linked to intention and then joined with deed is the basic ingredient of spellwork, and in magic, what "seems like" often "is." The underlying message of sympathetic magic is to trust your instincts, for if something intuitively seems right to you, it most often is.

The use of gemstones in ritual is perhaps the most vivid example of sympathetic magic. Just as each color gives off its own unique vibration, so does each gemstone seem to have a particular effect that often results from the combined nature of composition and color. The color associations that we make in our mind are embodied in gemstones, and this belief gives the gems part of their power. It should be noted that gemstones are natural elements from the earth and have their own inherent sacred energy that we seek to amplify by using them in spells or rituals. Gems are sacred in and of themselves, whether we choose to acknowledge them as such or not. Quartz is scientifically known to be a highly conductive substance, able to transmit great amounts of energy. How we choose to direct that energy through our intentions is the key to practicing effective magic.

To begin working with gems and crystals, it is important first to clear the stone of any residual energy present from someone who may have previously handled the gem. This can be accomplished in several ways. One of the easiest ways is to smudge the gem with a sage bundle. Smudging with sage is Native American in origin but is often used by modern witches because of its effectiveness. Sage leaves will smolder once the igniting flame has been blown out, leaving a pleasant smoke that burns like incense and is believed to remove unwanted vibrations from the surrounding environment. Light some sage and hold the gem or crystal over the rising smoke, turning it often so that all sides come into contact with the smoke. As the smoke rises and dissipates, so will the residual energy, leaving the stone clean and clear to be dedicated to a new purpose.

Another method of clearing a stone is to make a small pillow or sachet of sage leaves. This can easily be done by sewing two 3×3–inch squares of white cotton material together on three sides, forming a pocket. Turn the pocket right side out and fill it with herbs. Sew up the remaining side, and you have a perfect sachet for clearing crystals. Place the gem or crystal on the sachet and leave it exposed to direct sunlight, preferably outdoors or on a brightly lit windowsill. The solar energy acts as nondestructive fire in its purifying form. The stone is cleansed, but not damaged as it would be if exposed to actual fire.

Depending on the type of work you plan to do with your gem, you can also use moonlight to clear the stone. Follow the same instructions as with sunlight, but substitute the light of the full moon. Immersion in water is another method of clearing gems, preferably running water. If you have the good fortune to live near a clear and unpolluted stream or a brook, securely tie the stone with a string before dipping it in the water, or you may find yourself making an unwitting gift to the river. If you use water to cleanse very small gemstones, place them in a pouch and make sure you hold on to the pouch. It is best if the water comes into direct contact with the stones in order to achieve the desired results.

If you have tried all of the above methods and still feel as though your gem contains some kind of unwanted residual energy, you can effectively clear the gem by literally grounding it. This method is best used by people who own or have access to private property to ensure that the stone will remain undisturbed. Bury the gemstone in the earth on a full moon evening. The earth will absorb the energy contained in the crystal and as the moon wanes, this energy will dissipate. As the moon waxes, the gem will be prepared for dedication to its new purpose and it will retain the grounded energy of the earth. While this method requires patience because it is best to leave the gem undisturbed for the whole lunar month, it is recommended for gemstones that will be used for the more intense aspects of magic; for instance, a crystal ball intended for scrying.

Gemstone Correspondences

When choosing the type of gem appropriate for enhancing a ritual or spell, consider the psychic associations of the following stones:

Agate—Used for banishing fear, establishing courage, and discerning spiritual truth. Also associated with acceptance and raising consciousness.

Alexandrite—Used for promoting renewal of the self through emotional and physical well-being.

Amber—Used as a healing agent and as a grounding element. Thought to absorb negative energy, while radiating light and warmth. Often used as a protective stone.

A Witch's Grimoire

Amethyst—Used for stimulating spiritual and psychic awareness, also associated with clarity of thought and the invoking of mystic dreams. Used as a gateway to greater attunement with deity.

Apache Tear—Carried as a good luck charm. Also associated with contacting spirit guides.

Aquamarine—Used for calming the nerves, soothing the emotions, meditation, and for protection at sea.

Aventurine—Used for bringing good fortune, perception, and courage in dealing with people. A comforting stone. Stabilizes emotions.

Bloodstone—Used for spiritual cleansing, developing self confidence, and harmony.

Carnelian—Used for revealing past life experiences, stimulating, and focusing thoughts. Promotes well-being.

Citrine—Used for gaining control over the emotions, enhancing clarity of thought, and overcoming obstacles. An energizing stone. Believed to enhance intuition.

Coral—Used for maintaining focus during meditations and visualizations.

Diamond—Used for spiritual attunement; reflects the highest amount of white light.

Emerald—Used for prophecy and foresight, healing, prosperity, and repelling evil. Associated with improving memory and strengthening willpower.

Fluorite—Used for directing energy, grounding, and centering. Used for discerning reality behind illusions and waking the higher aspects of the mind.

Garnet—Used for enhancing the recollection of dreams, attracting love, and lifting the spirits.

Hematite—Used for grounding energy. Silvery black in appearance, but when scratched against a rough surface, it leaves a red stain, hence its association with blood.

Herkimer diamond—Double-terminated quartz. Considered a powerful transmitter of energy. Used for visions and dreams and for balancing oneself with higher forces.

Jade—Used for soothing the emotions, invoking peace, tranquility, and wisdom. Regarded as a symbol of good luck. Associated with courage, justice, wealth, and happiness. Used as an aid in increasing communication abilities, particularly the articulation of thoughts.

Jasper—Used for balancing the emotions and strengthening the will to do good works in the world. A healing stone. Opens the mind to new ways of thinking.

Jet—Used for protection, the elimination of fear, and counteracting depression.

Kunzite—Used for attuning with spiritual love vibrations and for attaining freedom from fear, soothing heartache, and increasing compassion.

Labradorite—Used for balancing the aura, attainment, and spiritual awareness.

Lapis lazuli—Used for attuning with deities, promoting fidelity, and enhancing friendships. Associated with stimulating creativity.

Malachite—Used to invoke prosperity. Represents inner peace, hope, healing, and protection.

Moonstone—Used for meditation, spiritual guidance, prophecy, love, and protection while traveling. Alleviates stress and helps control the emotions.

Obsidian—Used for balancing and calming the nerves.

Onyx—Used for releasing old habits and unwanted partnerships. Absorbs, then transforms negative energy.

Opal—Used for channeling, psychic journeys, chakra balancing, and divination.

Pearl—Used for enhancing wisdom and love relationships.

Peridot—Used for the development of inner vision and the healing of love relationships. Represents lightness and beauty. Associated with developing clairvoyance.

Quartz crystal—Used as a bridge between the material and the spiritual world and for meditation and transmitting energy. Used for healing, and thought to enhance the attributes of other stones it is worn or used with.

Rhodocrosite—Used for attracting love, healing the emotions, and inspiring forgiveness.

Rose quartz—Used for comfort and overcoming emotional instability. Associated with aiding love relationships.

Ruby—Used for enhancing mental concentration, augmenting confidence, and increasing spiritual wisdom. Associated with passion for life and truth.

Rutilated quartz—Used the same way as clearer quartz crystal. Some believe that the rutile inclusions enhance its effectiveness and aid the process of healing. Associated with mental stimulation.

Sapphire—Used for uncovering truth, aiding meditation, enhancing insight, calming the emotions, and attracting the good influence of others.

Smoky quartz—Used for attuning with nature, mental healing, and developing clairvoyant abilities. Associated with easing depression and realizing dreams.

Sodalite—Used for enhancing courage and endurance. Balances fears of the subconscious mind and assuages guilt. Associated with communication and self-expression.

Tiger's eye—Used for protection and purification. Focuses the mind and increases psychic ability.

Tourmaline—Used for balance and protection. Associated with grounding spiritual energies.

Turquoise—Used for enhancing friendships and empowering spiritual nature. A receptive stone. Used in channeling.

Zircon—Used as an aid in interpreting images and symbols, safety in travel, and communication with spirits.

Crystals and gems can be used in numerous ways to allow you to experience their metaphysical qualities:

- Wear gems on your body as jewelry to assist in bringing about a specific magical desire.
- Place them on your altar during a ritual so their energy aids the work at hand.
- Carry them in a pocket or a pouch as a charm to enhance a specific intention.
- Lay them directly on your body during meditation sessions to openly absorb the beneficial effects of their energy.

Crystals and gems can be used singly or in combination for many purposes. The color of a gem or a crystal gives a stone its unique desirability and links its energy to the intended effects. Consider the following color groups as a general guideline when selecting gems to use for spells, charms, and rituals.

Clear stones are generally associated with purification, including purification of physical, emotional, mental, and spiritual bodies.

Book of Lights and Shadows

Clear stones most closely resemble light, hence their purifying associations.

Red stones are generally associated with energy, courage, and sex. Red is associated with passion, so it follows to reason that stones of this hue would be regarded as enhancing energetic and sexual functions.

Pink stones are generally associated with love, self-esteem, and respect. Think of the passion of red balanced with the purity of white and it will be easy to see why stones of this color get their loving correlation.

Yellow stones are generally associated with mental awareness, emotional balance, and willpower. Think of the properties associated with the solar plexus chakra.

Orange stones are generally associated with cheerfulness and freedom from responsibility.

Green stones are generally associated with healing, growth, abundance, and self-control. Because the heart chakra is green, this color, along with pink, is also associated with love.

Light blue stones are generally associated with intuition and memory.

Dark blue stones are generally associated with protection, strength, and occult energies.

Violet and purple stones are generally associated with transformation and elevation of the spirit.

A Witch's Grimoire

Gold is generally associated with wisdom, self-confidence, and strengthening of the heart.

Brown stones are generally associated with stability and practicality.

Black stones are generally associated with protective energies, the material plane, and abstract thought.

While these descriptions are broad, they give you an overview of how to categorize and use gems to their best advantage by assessing their magical properties. You will come across many stones that you resonate with, and having a general idea of the energies associated with certain gem colors will assist you in using them properly. For example, if your intention is to heal a rift with a friend, you can choose to create a charm including emerald and lapis lazuli. If you want to mend a rift with a lover, you might choose rose quartz and peridot. If your intention is to amicably dissolve a relationship, onyx and jade might be a good combination. Use the worksheet that follows to assist yourself in making powerful choices that will aid your intentions through the use of gemstones.

Book of Lights and Shadows

Choosing Gemstones

Present situation

_____

_____

Desired change or effect

_____

_____

Gems chosen

_____

_____

Psychic associations

_____

_____

A Witch's Grimoire

Color associations

Manner in which gems are used or worn

9

Practical Applications
Walk the Path and Live a Spiritual Life

By now you may have come to look upon your grimoire as more than just another working tool. After all, there are few equally powerful methods of attaining self-awareness that can easily be used every day. The repository of your most private thoughts, spells, chants, and meditations will, at times, seem more like a friend than a book.

Think of all the information in your grimoire and give some thought as to how you would most like to organize your book. Do you intend to make it strictly chronological, with each entry in the order that you record it? Or, are you more comfortable dividing the grimoire into predetermined sections, keeping all spells together, all lists of ingredients together, all dream recordings together, etc.? The possibilities are so inspiring that one could even make a chant dedicated to the grimoire that could also serve as a table of contents or an introductory page:

A Witch's Grimoire

Magic.
History.
Biography.
Mystery.
Recipe.
Ecstasy.
Memory.
Prophecy.
Meditation;
Consecration.
Remembrance.
Ascendance.
Spells and charms;
Protection from harm.
Invocation.
Celebration.
Introspection
And reflection.
Blessed Moon,
Sacred rune,
Seasons turn,
Candles burn,
Lessons learned,
The Light returns.
In my hand of write
By day and night
In shadow or flame
The one constant is change.
Recorded now forevermore
Safe in the pages
Of a blessed grimoire.

Practical Applications

Use the worksheets included in this book as guides for developing your organizational strategy. Perhaps you will find that you want to copy the information from the worksheets directly into your book. You may discard other worksheets, depending on if the exercises were effective for you or not. Successful spells should always be recorded. Even spells that did not have the desired result should be recorded. That way, you can avoid repeating unsuccessful spells. You may even find that making a small adjustment to a previously unsuccessful spell may achieve the desired result after all.

There is no doubt that at some point you have experienced difficulty on your path. Whether this difficulty has been manifested through the lack of understanding or through the prejudice of others—or even in disagreements between like-minded individuals—there will be times when you will be challenged in life simply because you are living the way you choose. Having a consistent practice will give you strength through the difficult times. Keeping your book of shadows will remind you of who you are during moments of darkness and doubt. You will also be preserving memories for years to come.

One of the most important things to remember when dedicating yourself to the Wiccan path is that any expression of spirituality or religion should be something that enhances your life. Wicca should be a part of your life, and not an all-consuming endeavor that may alienate you from mundane reality and your earthly community. Overzealous witches can get so involved in meditations, consecrations, invocations, spells, and charms, rites, and rituals that there is little time or energy left for anything else. It is important to maintain a sense of balance in your practice, as well as in your life, so that you do not lose your connections to people and things. Remember the highly regarded priestesses of Delphi whose sacred oracle was inspired by the following maxims: Know Thyself

and

Moderation in All Things.

A Witch's Grimoire

The beauty of Wicca is that it essentially connects its devotees to the deities and to nature. The Goddess is alive and all around us. There are many simple things you can do to honor her through making conscious choices about how you live your life. Respecting and conserving natural resources is one way to honor and protect the earth, which Wiccans call Mother.

Take a good look at your life and you will find ways to maintain balance while making better choices that are aligned with your Wiccan beliefs. Consider buying a farmer's almanac to have a reference guide for lunar phases, seasonal changes, average rainfall, and a wealth of other information about the earth. Knowledge is power, and the more you learn about the earth, the more you will respect her, and the greater significance your magic will hold.

Take the time to use your grimoire on a regular basis. Incorporate writing into your magical practice. Find some time to write in the morning, remembering your dreams and delineating your hopes for the day. Think about the aspects of the day to come and how they may affect you. You can even keep a record of your daily horoscope and observe its accuracy. Find things that inspire you and include them. Press flowers between the pages. Paste in pictures of beloved ones or scenes that inspire you. Add a feather to remember the feeling of the wind on your face. Draw pictures. Do not limit your imagination!

Your grimoire can be anything and everything you want it to be. It is the place for you to explore and express your spirituality: a safe place where you will always be free from others' judgment, criticism, and skepticism. No one but you need be aware of the secrets kept within its pages if you wish. Write in the evening to reflect on the day's events. A line or two will suffice. Honor the forgotten moments in life by jotting down a word or two about the sunset or the fall of twilight. Keep track of your ritual preparations, and record your experiences after each rite.

Practical Applications

Final Notes

The resources listed in the Appendix, along with *A Witch's Grimoire*, may serve as guides along your spiritual path. By creating your own grimoire, you are becoming more aware of your magical life. Never stop learning, growing, and changing. Be passionate about yourself, even as you change, even in the face of the unknown. By writing your story, you may also become an inspiration for others. May your book of shadows deepen your knowledge of yourself, your aspirations, your dreams, and your loves. May it comfort you in times of darkness and bring you joy in times of light. May it hold your secrets as would a trusted friend, protect the stories of your lifetime, and hold your personal mythology securely. Merry meet, and merry part, and merry meet again. Blessed be.

Appendix

Sources for Obtaining Magical Ingredients

While your local grocery store or food co-op will certainly prove to be a treasure trove of magical ingredients, other tools of the craft may prove more difficult to find. If you are looking for a magnificent, top-of-the-line book of shadows with metal hinges and a locking mechanism, check out Brahms Bookworks at *www.brahmsbookworks.com*. Their books, while very expensive, are quite amazing. You can also contact them via mail order by writing to:

Robyn L. Ward
10726 Dalton Ave
Tampa, Fl 33615
(813) 855-7167

For a more affordable—but no less amazing—book of shadows, investigate the leather-bound, beautifully adorned books available from Capricorn's Lair. Their Web site is *www.capricornslair.com*. For mail inquiries, write to:

Capricorn's Lair
2450 Washington Blvd
Ogden, Utah 84401

And remember, when shopping for your grimoire, do not rule out your local bookstores and art supply stores as a resource for blank books.
For hard-to-find books, magical tools, and altar adornments, contact:

Enchantments
341 East Ninth Street
New York, NY 10003
(212) 228-4394

A Witch's Grimoire

Morgana's Chamber
242 West Tenth Street
New York, NY 10014
(212) 243-3415

For all necessary items related to candle magic, contact:

Other Worldly Waxes
131 East Seventh Street
New York, NY 10009
(212) 260-9188

For all manner of herbs and essential oils:

Angelica
147 First Avenue
New York, NY 10003
(212) 677-1549

Aphrodisia
264 Bleecker Street
New York, NY 10014
(212) 989-6440

For medical-grade essential oils:
Enfleurage
321 Bleecker St
New York, NY 10014
(212) 691-1610

Appendix

If you do not have a local Wiccan or New Age supply store in your area, consider obtaining your ritual tools online. The following Web sites offer an interesting array of items intended for magical purposes:

www.mysticearth.us Offers comprehensive Wicca and New Age supplies.

www.herbalmusings.com Here you will find certified organic herbs available in bulk, essential oils, and ritual supplies.

www.moonlightmysteries.com This Web site offers writing supplies such as quills, magical inks, and inkwells, as well as talismans and tools of the Craft.

www.awakethewitch.com You'll find vintage cauldrons, 1800s reproduction brooms, as well as other unique ritual tools.

These vendors will offer most everything you will need in order to maintain a quality supply of magical ingredients for all of your ritual purposes.

Suggested Reading

There are many books on the subject of Wicca and its related mythological origins. While this list is by no means complete, many of these books include extensive bibliographies that may lead you to new discoveries.

Any book by Scott Cunningham, Llewellyn Publications.

Advanced Astrology for Life, by Constance Stellas, Provenance Press, 2004.

Beyond God the Father, by Mary Daly, Beacon Press, 1973.

A Witch's Grimoire

Book of Shadows, by Phyllis Curott, Broadway Books, 1998.

Drawing Down the Moon, by Margot Adler, Beacon Press, 1979.

Eight Sabbats for Witches, by Janet and Stewart Farrar, Phoenix Publishing, 1981.

The Elements of the Celtic Tradition, by Caitlin Matthews, Thorsons/Element, 1990.

The Everything® Wicca & Witchcraft Book, by Marian Singer, Adams Media, 2002.

The Golden Ass, by Lucius Apuleius, translated by Robert Graves, Farrar, Strauss, and Giroux, 1951.

The Holy Book of Women's Mysteries, Vol I & II, by Z. Budapest, Wingbow, 1991.

Jambalaya, by Luisah Teish, Harper Collins, 1988.

Juno Covella: Perpetual Calendar of the Fellowship of Isis, by Lawrence Durdin-Robertson, Cesara Publications 1982.

Lady of the Beasts: Ancient Images of the Goddess and Her Sacred Animals, by Buffie Johnson, Harper San Francisco, 1981.

Laughter of Aphrodite, by Carol Christ, Harper & Row, 1987.

The Mists of Avalon, by Marion Zimmer Bradley, Ballantine Books, 1984.

Appendix

Motherpeace, by Vicki Noble, Harper San Francisco, 1983.

The Mysteries of Isis, by deTraci Regula, Llewellyn Publications, 1996.

The Power of Myth, by Joseph Campbell, Broadway Books, 1988.

Priestesses, by Norma Lorre Goodrich, Harper Collins, 1990.

Rituals for Life, by Brenda Knight, Provenance Press, 2004.

The Sea Priestess and *Moon Magic*, or any other books by Dion Fortune, Weiser Books.

The Search for Omm Sety, by Jonathon Cott, Warner Books Incorporated, 1989.

The Spiral Dance, by Starhawk, Harper & Row, 1979.

When God Was a Woman: Ancient Mirrors of Womanhood, by Merlin Stone, Harcourt, Brace, Jovanovich, 1976.

The White Goddess, by Robert Graves, Farrar, Strauss, and Giroux, 1948.

The Women's Encyclopedia of Myths and Secrets, by Barbara Walker, Harper Collins, 1983.

Selected Bibliography

A Medieval Herbal. Chronicle Books. San Francisco, California. 1994.

Berger, Judith. *Herbal Rituals*. St. Martin's Press. New York, New York. 1998.

Blum, Ralph. *The Book of Runes*. St. Martin's Press. New York, New York. 1982.

Bruce, Margaret. *The Little Grimoire*. The Angel Press. Durham, England. 1965.

Buckland, Raymond. *Buckland's Complete Book of Witchcraft*. Llewellyn Publications. St. Paul, Minnesota. 1986.

Buckland, Raymond. *The Tree: The Complete Book of Saxon Witchcraft*. Samuel Weiser. New York, New York. 1974.

Budapest, Zsuzsanna. *The Grandmother of Time: A Women's Book of Celebrations, Spells, and Sacred Objects for Every Month of the Year*. Harper and Row. San Francisco, California. 1989.

Campanelli, Pauline. *Ancient Ways: Reclaiming Pagan Traditions*. Llewellyn Publications. St. Paul, Minnesota. 1991.

Cresta. *Faerye Invokation*. Ars Obscura. Seattle, Washington. 1981.

Crowley, Vivianne. *Phoenix from the Flame: Living as a Pagan in the 21st Century*. Thorsons, Harper Collins. San Francisco, California. 1995.

Appendix

Cunningham, Scott. *The Magic in Food: Legends, Lore, and Spells.* Llewellyn Publications. St. Paul, Minnesota. 1992.

Dunwich, Gerina. *The Magic of Candle Burning.* Citadel Press. New York, New York. 1989.

Eisler, Riane. *The Chalice and the Blade: Our History, Our Future.* Harper and Row. San Francisco, California. 1988.

Farrar, Janet and Stewart. *The Witches' Way.* Phoenix Publishing. Custer, Washington. 1984.

Fitch, Ed. *A Grimoire of Shadows.* Llewellyn Publications. St. Paul, Minnesota. 1996.

Fitch, Ed. *The Rites of Odin.* Llewellyn Publications. St. Paul, Minnesota. 1990.

Flowers, Stephen. *The Galdrabòk: An Icelandic Grimoire.* Samuel Weiser. New York, New York. 1989.

Fortune, Dion. *Psychic Self-Defence.* Samuel Weiser. New York, New York. 1930.

Frost, Gavin and Yvonne. *A Witch's Grimoire of Ancient Omens, Portents, Talismans, Amulets, and Charms.* Godolphin House Publishers. Hinton, West Virginia. 1976.

Gardner-Gordon, Joy. *Pocket Guide to Chakras.* The Crossing Press. Freedom, California. 1998.

Garfield, Patricia. *The Universal Dream Key*. Cliff Street Books, Harper Collins. New York, New York. 2001.

Golden, Alisa. *Creating Handmade Books*. Sterling Publishing. New York, New York. 1998.

Goodman, Linda. *Linda Goodman's Love Signs*. Ballantine Books. New York, New York. 1978.

Graves, Robert. *The White Goddess*. Farrar, Straus, and Giroux. New York, New York. 1948.

http://wiccachile.tripod.com

Leland, Charles G. *Aradia: Gospel of the Witches*. Phoenix Publishing. Custer, Washington. 1990.

McCarthy, Mary and Manna, Philip. *Making Books by Hand*. Quarry Books. Gloucester, Massachusetts. 2000.

Mestel, Sherry. *Earth Rites, Volume Two: Rituals*. Earth Rites Press. New York, New York. 1978.

Millidge, Judith. *The Handbook of Dreams: How to Interpret and Understand your Dreams*. Barnes and Noble. New York, New York. 2004.

Morrison, Dorothy. *The Craft: A Witch's Book of Shadows*. Llewellyn Publications. St. Paul, Minnesota. 2003.

Paper Craft. North Light Books. Cincinnati, Ohio. 1993.

Appendix

Riggs-Bergesen, Catherine. *Candle Therapy: A Magical Guide to Life Enhancement.* Andrews McMeel Publishing. Kansas City, Missouri. 2003.

Robertson, Olivia. *Sybil: Oracles of the Goddess.* Cesara Publications. Enniscorthy, Ireland. 1989.

Sabrina, Lady. *The Witches Master Grimoire: An Encyclopedia of Charms, Spells, Formulas, and Magical Rites.* New Page Books. Franklin Lakes, New Jersey. 2001.

Starhawk. *The Spiral Dance: A Rebirth of the Ancient Religion of the Great Goddess.* Harper and Row. San Francisco, California. 1979.

Starsky, Stella and Cox, Quinn. *Sextrology: The Astrology of Sex and the Sexes.* HarperResource, Harper Collins. New York, New York. 2004.

Stein, Diane. *The Women's Spirituality Book.* Llewellyn Publications. St. Paul, Minnesota. 1986.

Stone, Merlin. *When God Was a Woman.* Harcourt Brace Jovanovich. San Diego, New York, London. 1976.

Wolkstein, Diane and Kramer, Samuel Noah. *Inanna Queen of Heaven and Earth.* Harper and Row. New York, New York. 1983.

Index

A
air, 39–41
alphabets, ceremonial, 21–24
altars, 25
Aquarius, 165
Aries, 158
aspecting, 180–87
athame, 60–61
autumnal equinox, 145

B
banishing spell, 70–73
Barley Moon, 153–54
Beltane, 146–47
between the worlds, 172–73
blessing, of grimoire, 18–20
Blood Moon, 155
book binding, 15–18
book of shadows, 2; *see also* grimoires
bread recipe, 50–54
breathing meditations, 96–98, 116–21
Brigid (goddess), 180

C
Cancer, 160
candle magic, 192–97
Candlemas, 146
Capricorn, 164
chakras, 88–96
chalices, 61–62
change, 167–68
channeling, 187–89
chanting, 171
Charge of the Goddess, 137–39
charm casting, 57–58
circles: casting, 32, 56; four directions and, 33–38; opening, 47–49
Cold Moon, 150
colors, 200–201, 217, 224–26
creative visualization, 80–88
cross-quarter days, 146–48
crown chakra, 95–96
crystal balls, 174–77

D
dancing, 172
dandelion blossom oil, 204–5
Dark Moon, 156
days of week, 103–8
deities, invocation of, 57
Dianic witchcraft, 137–38
directions: invocation of four, 33–38; releasing, 47–49
dreams: allowing Goddess in during, 116–21; imagination and, 113–14; interpretation of, 122–33; recording, 114–16, 133
drums, 170–71

E
earth, 45–47
east, 33, 35–36, 49
elder flower water, 206
elemental powers: awakening the, 39–47; combining, in sacred spiral, 50–54; of the four directions, 33–38; releasing, 47–49
Embracing the Flame (spell), 42–43
equinoxes, 142–45
esbats, 148–66; full moon, 149–56; new moon, 157–66
essential oils, 199–200, 204–5
evening rites, 111–13

F
Faerie Runes, 23–24
fire, 41–43
flower water, 199, 206
Friday, 107–8
full moon, 149–56
Futhark Runes, 22–23

244

Index

G
Gemini, 159
gemstones, 217–28
Goddess, ix, 4. *See also specific goddesses*;
  aspects of the, 180–82; Charge of the, 137–39; myths about, 141; names for, 182–85
Great Wheel, 141–42
grimoires: consecration of, 18–20; construction of, 10–18; defined, 1–4; organization of, 229–31; origins of, 5–7; reasons for writing, 4–5, 231–32; types of, 9–10
grounding technique, 26–28

H
Hare Moon, 151–52
Harvest Moon, 154
heart chakra, 92
herbs, 197–216

I
imagination, 113–14
Imbolc, 146
Inanna (goddess), 5–6
incense, 30–31
imitation, 5
Ishtar (goddess), 6
Isis (goddess), 6–7

K
Knowth, 143
kundalini, 89

L
Lammastide, 147
lavender bath salts, 208
Leo, 160–61
Libra, 162
Litha, 145
Lugnasadh, 147

M
Mabon, 145
magic: candle, 192–97; of change, 167–68; sympathetic, 217–19; theory and practice of, 55–58; tools for, 58–64, 64–66
mantras, 99–101
May Day, 146–47
Mead Moon, 152–53
meditation, 96–101
mirrors, black, 177
Monday, 104–5
moon: full, 149–56; new, 157–66
morning rites, 109–11
mugwort dream pillow, 210
Muses, 180–81

N
Newgrange, 143
new moon, 157–66
north, 34–35, 38, 47–48

O
Older Rune Row, 22–23
Osiris (god), 6–7
Ostara, 144

P
papermaking, 10–14
pentacles, 62–63
Pisces, 165–66
preparation: for magical work, 56; ritual, 26–28
protection spell, 68–70

R
Raising the Wind (spell), 39–41
reality, suspension of, 79, 170
record gathering, 20–21
relaxation techniques, 26–28
rhymes, 73

Index

rituals, 29; evening, 111–13; morning, 109–11; preparation for, 26–28
ritual spaces. *See* sacred space
root chakra, 89–90
runes, 22–24

S
sabbats, 142–45
sacral chakra, 90–91
sacred space, 25, 29–32
Sagittarius, 163
Samhain, 148
Saturday, 108
Scorpio, 162–63
scrying, 173–79
seasons, 141–45
Seed Moon, 151
sistrum, 171–72
Snow Moon, 155–56
solar plexus chakra, 91
solstices, 142–45
Song of Amergin, 139–40
sound, using in meditation, 98–101
south, 33–34, 36–37, 48–49
spells: casting, 56–57; crafting own, 73–78; practical application of, 66–73; *see also specific spells*
spring equinox, 144
Star of David, 169–70
Stonehenge, 143
Storm Moon, 150–51
summer solstice, 145
Sunday, 104
symbols, 58, 169–70
sympathetic magic, 217–19

T
Taurus, 158–59
temple sleep, 116–21
Theban Alphabet, 21–22
third eye chakra, 94–95

throat chakra, 93–94
Thursday, 107
tools: consecration of, 64–66; for magical work, 58–64; for scrying, 174–78; of the trance, 170–72
trance, 168–73
Triple Goddess, 180
Tuesday, 105–6

V
Virgo, 161
visualization, creative, 80–88

W
wands, 59–60
washing spell, 66–68
water, 43–45, 178
Waters of the Moon (spell), 44–45
Wednesday, 106
west, 34, 37, 48
Wheel of the Year, 141–42
Wicca, 3, 4, 7–9
Wiccan Rede, 135–37
Wild Moon, 150
winter solstice, 144
Wort Moon, 153

Y
Yule, 144